SCIENTIFIC PROGRESS GOES "BOINK"

Also by Bill Watterson

CALVIN AND HOBBES
SOMETHING UNDER THE BED IS DROOLING
YUKON HO!
WEIRDOS FROM ANOTHER PLANET
THE REVENGE OF THE BABY-SAT
THE CALVIN AND HOBBES LAZY SUNDAY BOOK
THE AUTHORITATIVE CALVIN AND HOBBES
ATTACK OF THE DERANGED MUTANT KILLER MONSTER SNOW GOONS
THE INDISPENSABLE CALVIN AND HOBBES
THE DAYS ARE JUST PACKED
HOMICIDAL PSYCHO JUNGLE CAT

SCIENTIFIC PROGRESS GOES "BOINK"

A Calvin and Hobbes Collection by Bill Watterson

WARNER BOOKS

A *Warner* Book

First published in the USA by Andrews and McMeel 1991
First published in Great Britain by Sphere Books Ltd 1991
Reprinted 1991
Reprinted by Warner Books 1992
Reprinted 1993 (twice), 1994, 1995

Printed and bound in Great Britain by
BPC Hazell Books Ltd
A member of
The British Printing Company Ltd

ISBN 0 7515 0481 5

Warner Books
A Division of
Little, Brown and Company (UK)
Brettenham House
Lancaster Place
London WC2E 7EN

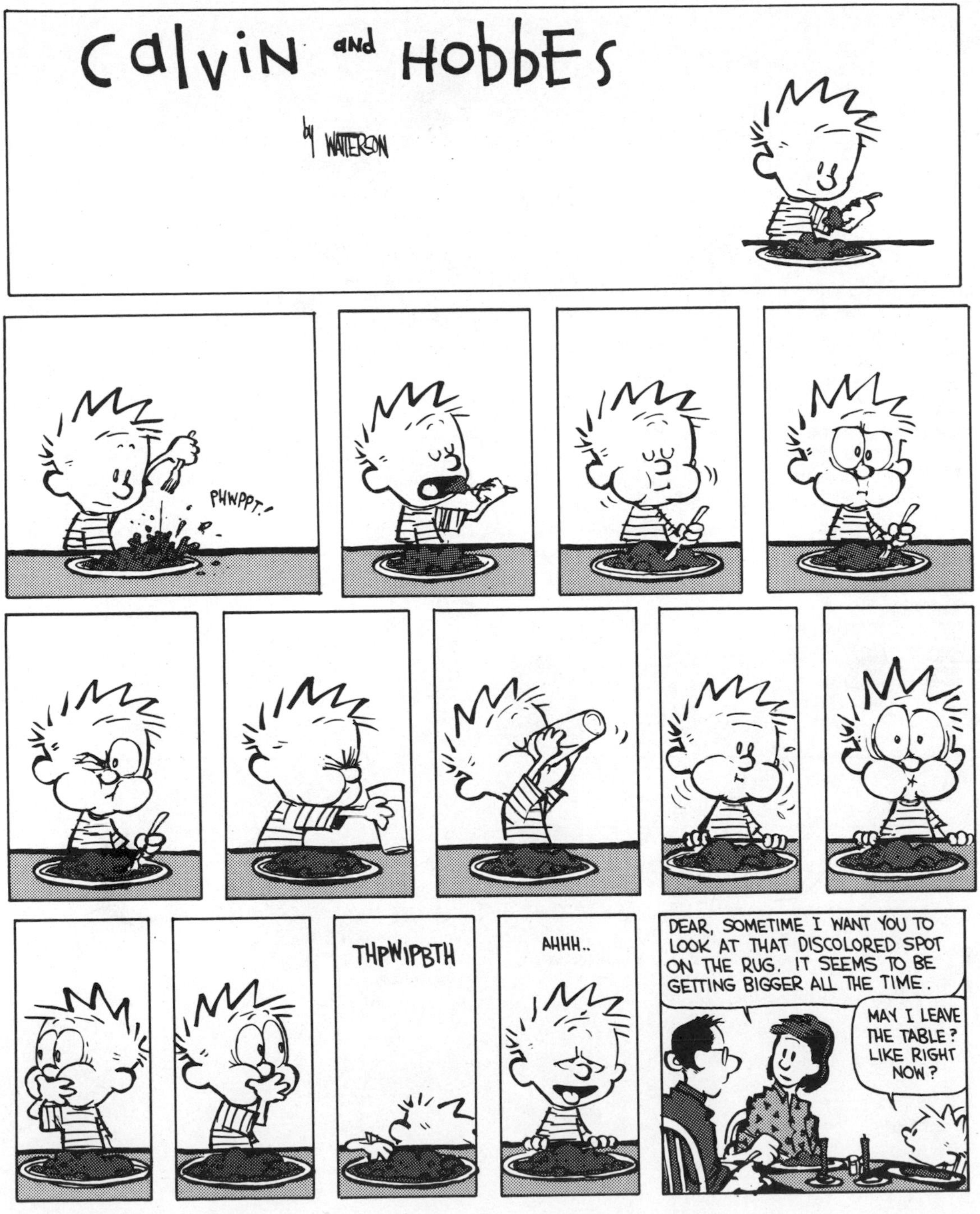
Calvin and HOBBES
by WATTERSON
PHWPPT!
THPWIPBTH
AHHH..
DEAR, SOMETIME I WANT YOU TO LOOK AT THAT DISCOLORED SPOT ON THE RUG. IT SEEMS TO BE GETTING BIGGER ALL THE TIME.
MAY I LEAVE THE TABLE? LIKE RIGHT NOW?

I want that truck, Twinky.

IT'S MINE, MOE. I BROUGHT IT FROM HOME.

I said gimme the truck.

MOE, YOU CAN'T JUST *TAKE* THINGS FROM PEOPLE BECAUSE YOU'RE BIGGER!

I'm not taking it. You're **giving** it to me because we'll both be so much happier that way.

HOW TOUCHING.

MOE, GIVE ME MY TRUCK BACK. IT'S NOT YOURS.

It is **now**. You gave it to me.

I DIDN'T HAVE MUCH CHOICE, *DID* I ?! IT WAS EITHER GIVE UP THE TRUCK OR GET PUNCHED!

So?

SO I ONLY "GAVE" IT TO YOU BECAUSE YOU'RE BIGGER AND MEANER THAN ME!

Yeah? ..."So?"

THE FORENSIC MARVEL HAS REDUCED MY LOGIC TO SHAMBLES.

You're saying you changed your mind about getting punched?

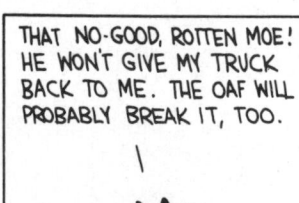

THAT NO-GOOD, ROTTEN MOE! HE WON'T GIVE MY TRUCK BACK TO ME. THE OAF WILL PROBABLY BREAK IT, TOO.

SHOULD I STEAL IT BACK? I KNOW STEALING IS WRONG, BUT *HE* STOLE IT FROM *ME*, AND IF I **DON'T** STEAL IT BACK, MOE WILL JUST KEEP IT, AND THAT'S NOT FAIR.

THEY SAY TWO WRONGS DON'T MAKE A RIGHT, BUT WHAT ARE YOU SUPPOSED TO *DO* THEN? JUST LET THE BIGGEST GUY MAKE HIS OWN RULES ALL THE TIME? LET MIGHT MAKE RIGHT?

...THAT SOUNDS REASONABLE.

BY GOLLY, I *AM* GOING TO STEAL MY TRUCK BACK FROM MOE! IT'S MINE AND HE HAS NO RIGHT TO HAVE IT!

I'LL JUST SNEAK UP BEHIND THE SWINGS HERE, AND WHEN MOE'S NOT LOOKING, I'LL RUN UP, GRAB THE TRUCK AND TAKE OFF!

THIS PLAYGROUND SHOULD HAVE ONE OF THOSE AUTOMATIC INSURANCE MACHINES LIKE THEY HAVE IN AIRPORTS.

OK, MOE'S GOT HIS BACK TO ME! NOW I'LL ZIP OVER, STEAL MY TRUCK BACK AND RUN LIKE CRAZY!

HE'LL NEVER KNOW WHAT HIT HIM! BY THE TIME HE SEES THE TRUCK IS GONE, I'LL BE A MILE AWAY! IT'S A FAIL-PROOF PLAN! NOTHING CAN GO WRONG! IT'S A SNAP!

THERE'S NO REASON TO HESITATE. IT'LL BE OVER IN A SPLIT SECOND, AND I'LL SURE BE GLAD TO HAVE MY TRUCK BACK! I'LL JUST DO IT AND BE DONE! NOTHING TO IT! IT'S EASY!

OBVIOUSLY MY BODY DOESN'T BELIEVE A WORD MY BRAIN IS SAYING.

PHOOEY, WHO AM I KIDDING? I'D NEVER GET AWAY WITH STEALING MY TRUCK BACK FROM MOE. THE UGLY GALOOT IS THE SIZE OF A BUICK.

HMM... SINCE I CAN'T *FIGHT* HIM, MAYBE I SHOULD TRY *TALKING* TO HIM. MAYBE IF I REASONED WITH HIM, HE'D SEE *MY* SIDE.

MAYBE HE'D REALIZE THAT STEALING HURTS PEOPLE, AND MAYBE HE'D RETURN MY TRUCK *WILLINGLY*.

MAYBE IF I'M REALLY LUCKY I WON'T GO THROUGH LIFE WITH THE NICKNAME "OMELET FACE."

7

CalviN and HobbEs

by WATTERSON

HAVE YOU SEEN MY SHOES? I THOUGHT I HAD THEM OUT RIGHT HERE.

YOUR SHOES? I DON'T KNOW.

THEY *WERE* RIGHT HERE. WHERE COULD THEY HAVE GONE?

WE'RE GOING TO BE LATE.

WELL I CAN'T GO ANYWHERE WITHOUT MY *SHOES.* HELP ME LOOK.

THEY'RE NOT LEAVING *US* WITH A BABY SITTER TONIGHT!

DING DONG

IT'S *ROSALYN!*

ANSWER THE DOOR, WILL YOU PLEASE, CALVIN?

HI ROZ. MY PARENTS CHANGED THEIR MINDS ABOUT GOING OUT, SO WE WON'T BE NEEDING YOUR SERVICES. GOODBYE.

HI, ROSALYN. WHAT ARE YOU TALKING ABOUT, CALVIN?

YOU CAN'T GO OUT IF MOM CAN'T FIND HER *SHOES,* RIGHT?

AND WHAT DO *YOU* KNOW ABOUT *THAT?*

I'D LIKE TO BE PAID IN ADVANCE TONIGHT.

UH, NOTHING! HA HA! UM, WHY? ARE HER SHOES MISSING?

PHOOEY. MOM AND DAD LEFT. NOW WE'RE HERE ALONE WITH THE BABY SITTER FROM THE BLACK LAGOON.

HEE HEE! DO YOU THINK SHE REMEMBERS HOW LAST TIME WE THREATENED TO FLUSH HER SCIENCE NOTES DOWN THE TOILET?

HA HA HA! OUR FINEST MOMENT!

OK, YOU, GET IN BED.

WHAT?! IT'S NOT EVEN 6:30!

SHE REMEMBERS, ALL RIGHT.

SHE CAN'T GET AWAY WITH THIS. WE'LL CALL THE RESCUE SQUAD.

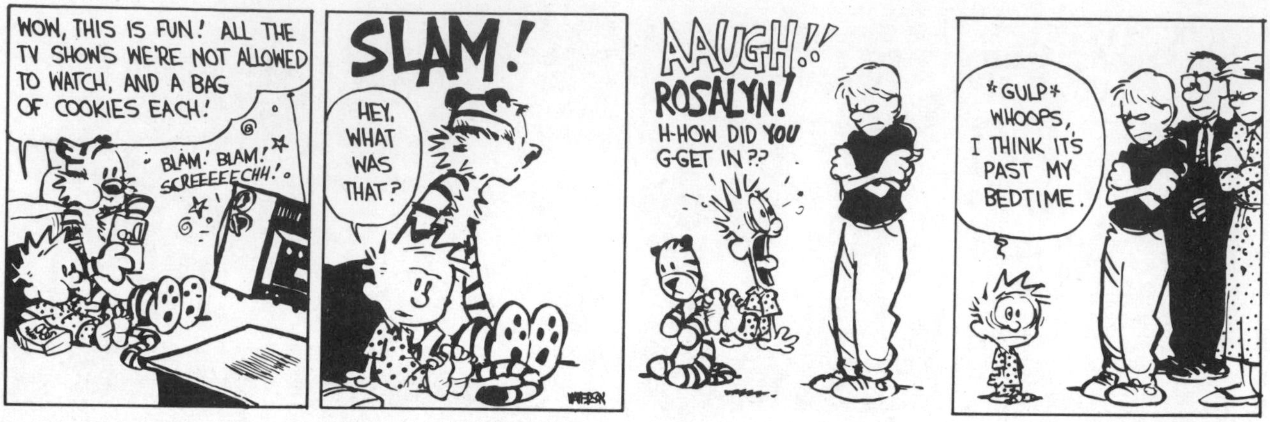
WOW, THIS IS FUN! ALL THE TV SHOWS WE'RE NOT ALLOWED TO WATCH, AND A BAG OF COOKIES EACH!
BLAM! BLAM! SCREEEEECHH!
SLAM!
HEY, WHAT WAS THAT?
AAUGH!!
ROSALYN!
H-HOW DID YOU G-GET IN??
GULP WHOOPS, I THINK IT'S PAST MY BEDTIME.

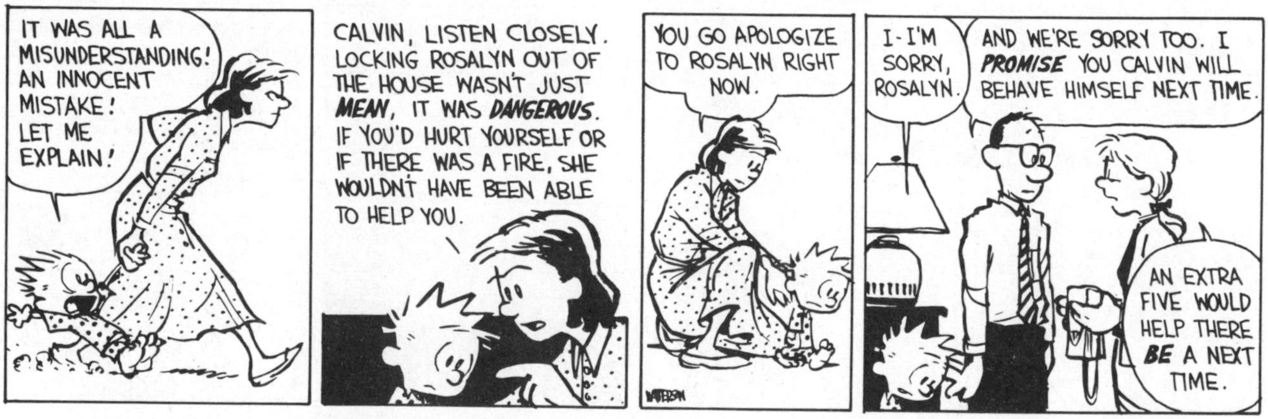
IT WAS ALL A MISUNDERSTANDING! AN INNOCENT MISTAKE! LET ME EXPLAIN!
CALVIN, LISTEN CLOSELY. LOCKING ROSALYN OUT OF THE HOUSE WASN'T JUST MEAN, IT WAS DANGEROUS. IF YOU'D HURT YOURSELF OR IF THERE WAS A FIRE, SHE WOULDN'T HAVE BEEN ABLE TO HELP YOU.
YOU GO APOLOGIZE TO ROSALYN RIGHT NOW.
I-I'M SORRY, ROSALYN.
AND WE'RE SORRY TOO. I PROMISE YOU CALVIN WILL BEHAVE HIMSELF NEXT TIME.
AN EXTRA FIVE WOULD HELP THERE BE A NEXT TIME.

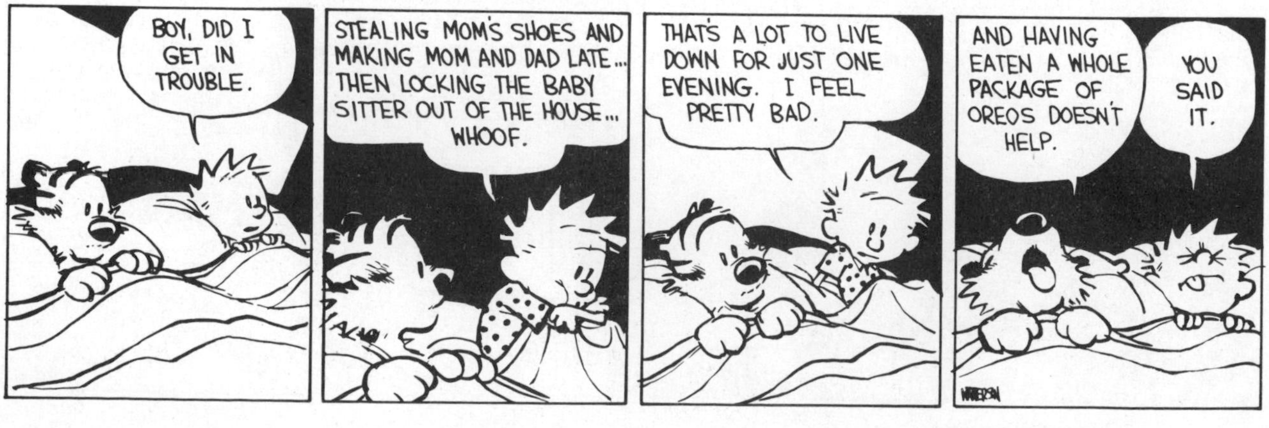
BOY, DID I GET IN TROUBLE.
STEALING MOM'S SHOES AND MAKING MOM AND DAD LATE... THEN LOCKING THE BABY SITTER OUT OF THE HOUSE... WHOOF.
THAT'S A LOT TO LIVE DOWN FOR JUST ONE EVENING. I FEEL PRETTY BAD.
AND HAVING EATEN A WHOLE PACKAGE OF OREOS DOESN'T HELP.
YOU SAID IT.

CALVIN and HOBBES

by WATTERSON

GISZH!... GISZH!...

15

STUPENDOUS MAN CIRCLES THE EARTH WITH A 200-INCH TELESCOPE LENS!

ALIGNED PERFECTLY WITH THE SUN, THE MAGNIFYING LENS FOCUSES THE TERRIBLE SOLAR ENERGY...

...AND FRIES A CERTAIN ELEMENTARY SCHOOL CLEAN OFF THE MAP!

NOW MILD-MANNERED CALVIN HAS NO NEED TO DO HIS HOMEWORK EVER AGAIN! LIBERTY PREVAILS!

HOW'S YOUR HOMEWORK COMING, CALVIN?

UH OH, IT'S MY ARCH-NEMESIS, MOM-LADY! SHE CAN'T DISCOVER MY SECRET IDENTITY!

CALVIN? ARE YOU DOING YOUR HOMEWORK IN THERE?

QUICKLY, STUPENDOUS MAN LEAPS INTO THE CLOSET TO CHANGE BACK INTO HIS 6-YEAR-OLD ALTER EGO, MILD-MANNERED CALVIN!

CALVIN? ARE YOU IN HERE?

UNFORTUNATELY, STUPENDOUS MAN'S CAPE IS CAUGHT IN MILD-MANNERED CALVIN'S ZIPPER! CURSES!

THIS IS GOING TO BE A GOOD ONE, I CAN TELL.

GEEZ, MOM! CAN'T A GUY HAVE A LITTLE PRIVACY?!

AND WHY, MAY I ASK, ARE YOU STANDING IN YOUR UNDERWEAR IN THE CLOSET?

OH, NO REASON. UM... I WAS HOT.

YOU'RE SUPPOSED TO BE DOING YOUR HOMEWORK!

I DON'T NEED TO DO IT NOW, THANKS TO STUPENDOUS MAN!

OH YEAH?

IT WAS GREAT! HE FRIED THE SCHOOL WITH A BIG MAGNIFYING LENS IN SPACE! I'M SURE IT WILL BE IN ALL THE PAPERS TOMORROW.

BOY, SHE'LL BE IN TROUBLE WHEN SHE GIVES ME MY COSTUME BACK. BIG TROUBLE.

I'VE GOT AN IDEA, DAD.

MAYBE I'D GET BETTER GRADES IF YOU OFFERED ME $1 FOR EVERY "D", $5 FOR EVERY "C", $10 FOR EVERY "B", AND $50 FOR EVERY "A"!

I'M NOT GOING TO *BRIBE* YOU, CALVIN. YOU SHOULD APPLY YOURSELF FOR YOUR OWN GOOD.

RATS. I THOUGHT I COULD MAKE AN EASY FOUR BUCKS.

HELLO? VALLEY HARDWARE? YES, I'M CALLING TO SEE IF YOU SELL BLASTING CAPS, DETONATORS, TIMERS AND WIRE.

JUST THE WIRE? OK, FORGET IT. DO YOU RENT BULLDOZERS OR BACKHOES?

NO, NO, A ROTOTILLER WON'T DO AT ALL. I NEED SOMETHING MORE LIKE A WRECKING BALL. DO YOU KNOW WHERE I COULD GET ANYTHING LIKE THAT? NO? OK, GOODBYE.

LOOKS LIKE ANOTHER BORING DAY, HOBBES.

I CAN'T SLEEP, HOBBES. I'VE BEEN THINKING.

WHAT ABOUT?

WELL, SUPPOSE THERE'S NO AFTERLIFE. THAT WOULD MEAN *THIS* LIFE IS ALL YOU GET.

AND *THAT* WOULD MEAN I'M SITTING HERE IN BED AS PRECIOUS MOMENTS OF MY ALL-TOO-SHORT LIFE DISAPPEAR FOREVER.

HONEY, WAKE UP. DO YOU HEAR THE TELEVISION ON?

20

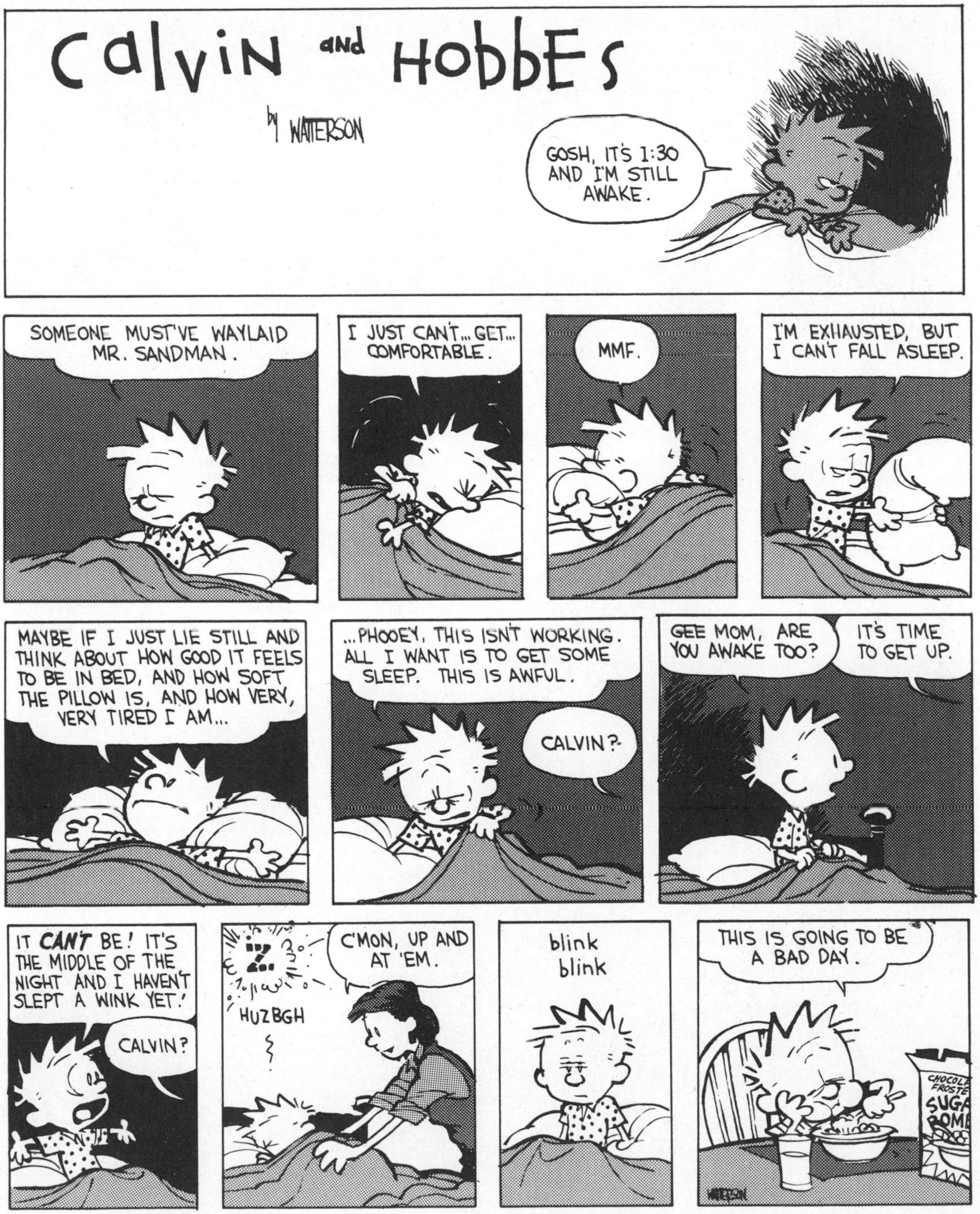
Calvin and Hobbes
by WATTERSON
GOSH, IT'S 1:30 AND I'M STILL AWAKE.
SOMEONE MUST'VE WAYLAID MR. SANDMAN.
I JUST CAN'T... GET... COMFORTABLE.
MMF.
I'M EXHAUSTED, BUT I CAN'T FALL ASLEEP.
MAYBE IF I JUST LIE STILL AND THINK ABOUT HOW GOOD IT FEELS TO BE IN BED, AND HOW SOFT THE PILLOW IS, AND HOW VERY, VERY TIRED I AM...
...PHOOEY, THIS ISN'T WORKING. ALL I WANT IS TO GET SOME SLEEP. THIS IS AWFUL.
CALVIN?
GEE MOM, ARE YOU AWAKE TOO?
IT'S TIME TO GET UP.
IT CAN'T BE! IT'S THE MIDDLE OF THE NIGHT AND I HAVEN'T SLEPT A WINK YET!
CALVIN?
Z
HUZBGH
C'MON, UP AND AT 'EM.
blink
blink
THIS IS GOING TO BE A BAD DAY.
WATTERSON

CaLViN and HObbEs

by WATTERSON

WOW, HONEY, YOU'RE MISSING A BEAUTIFUL SUNSET OUT HERE!

I'LL COUNT TO 10, AND THEN... POW!

DAD, HOW COME OLD PHOTOGRAPHS ARE ALWAYS BLACK AND WHITE? DIDN'T THEY HAVE COLOR FILM BACK THEN?

SURE THEY DID. IN FACT, THOSE OLD PHOTOGRAPHS *ARE* IN COLOR. IT'S JUST THE *WORLD* WAS BLACK AND WHITE THEN.

REALLY?

YEP. THE WORLD DIDN'T TURN COLOR UNTIL SOMETIME IN THE 1930s, AND IT WAS PRETTY GRAINY COLOR FOR A WHILE, TOO.

THAT'S REALLY WEIRD.

WELL, TRUTH IS STRANGER THAN FICTION.

BUT THEN WHY ARE OLD *PAINTINGS* IN COLOR?! IF THE WORLD WAS BLACK AND WHITE, WOULDN'T ARTISTS HAVE PAINTED IT THAT WAY?

NOT NECESSARILY, A LOT OF GREAT ARTISTS WERE INSANE.

BUT...BUT HOW COULD THEY HAVE PAINTED IN COLOR ANYWAY? WOULDN'T THEIR PAINTS HAVE BEEN SHADES OF GRAY BACK THEN?

OF COURSE, BUT THEY TURNED COLORS LIKE EVERYTHING ELSE DID IN THE '30s.

SO WHY DIDN'T OLD BLACK AND WHITE PHOTOS TURN COLOR TOO?

BECAUSE THEY WERE COLOR PICTURES OF BLACK AND WHITE, REMEMBER?

THE WORLD IS A COMPLICATED PLACE, HOBBES.

WHENEVER IT SEEMS THAT WAY, I TAKE A NAP IN A TREE AND WAIT FOR DINNER.

PAY ATTENTION TO ME.

I'VE GOT TO WRITE A REPORT FOR SCHOOL.

WHAT'S YOUR TOPIC?

BATS. CAN YOU IMAGINE ANYTHING MORE STUPID?

HECK, *I* DON'T KNOW ANYTHING ABOUT BATS! HOW AM I SUPPOSED TO WRITE A REPORT ON A SUBJECT I KNOW NOTHING ABOUT?! IT'S IMPOSSIBLE!

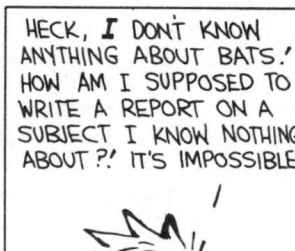

I SUPPOSE RESEARCH IS OUT OF THE QUESTION.

OH, LIKE I'M GOING TO LEARN ABOUT BATS AND *THEN* WRITE A REPORT?! GIVE ME A BREAK!

HELLO, SUSIE? THIS IS CALVIN. YOU KNOW THIS REPORT WE'RE SUPPOSED TO WRITE FOR SCHOOL? YEAH. MY TOPIC IS BATS. WHAT'S YOURS?

ELEPHANTS? HMM. WELL, ARE YOU GOING TO THE LIBRARY TO LOOK UP ELEPHANTS? YOU ARE? GREAT!

WHILE YOU'RE THERE, COULD YOU RESEARCH BATS TOO, AND MAKE COPIES OF ALL THE INFORMATION YOU FIND, AND MAYBE UNDERLINE THE IMPORTANT PARTS FOR ME, AND SORT OF OUTLINE IT, SO I WOULDN'T HAVE TO READ IT ALL?

HOW'D IT GO?

I REALLY LOATHE GIRLS.

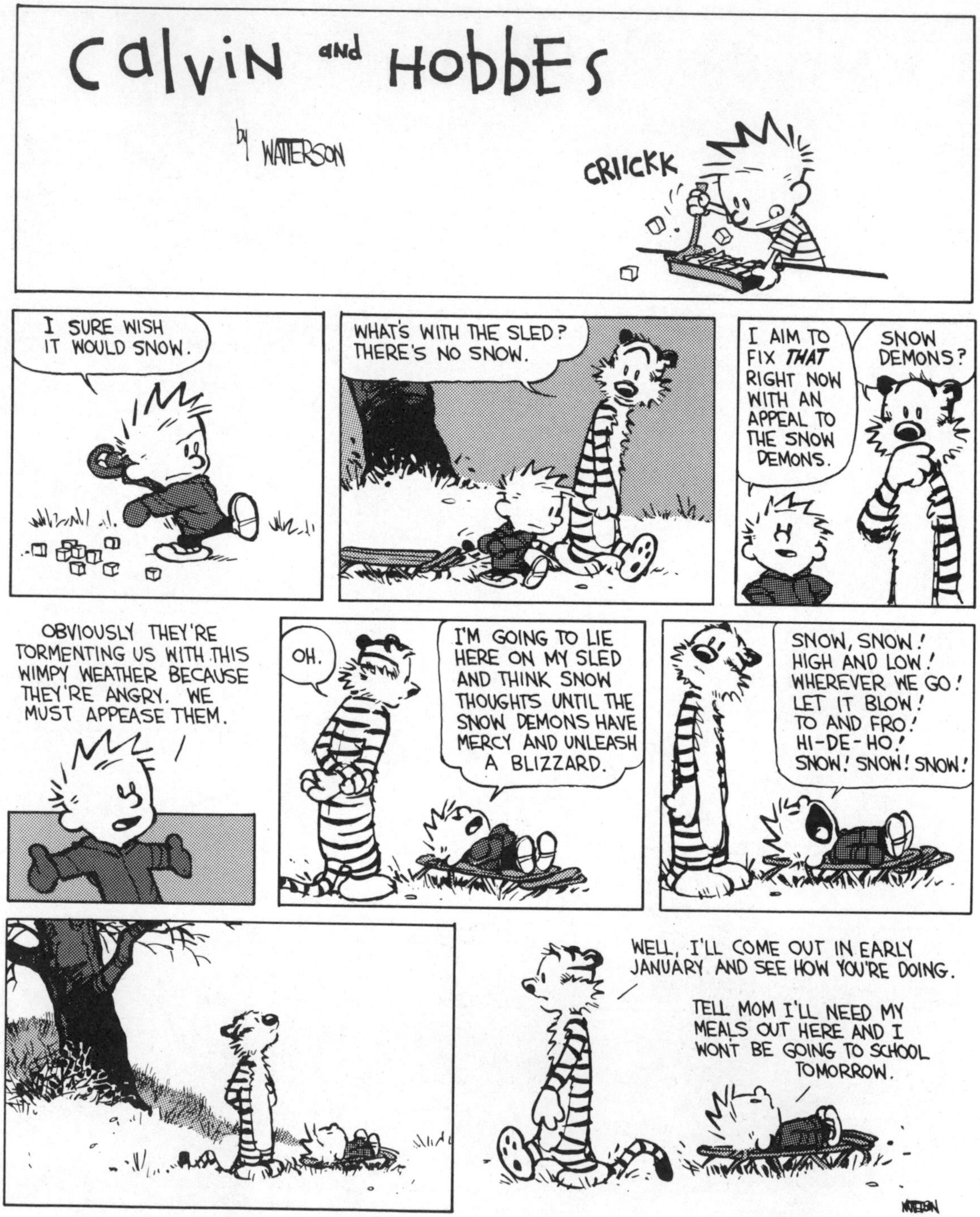
Calvin and HOBBES
by WATTERSON
CRICKK
I SURE WISH IT WOULD SNOW.
WHAT'S WITH THE SLED? THERE'S NO SNOW.
I AIM TO FIX THAT RIGHT NOW WITH AN APPEAL TO THE SNOW DEMONS.
SNOW DEMONS?
OBVIOUSLY THEY'RE TORMENTING US WITH THIS WIMPY WEATHER BECAUSE THEY'RE ANGRY. WE MUST APPEASE THEM.
OH.
I'M GOING TO LIE HERE ON MY SLED AND THINK SNOW THOUGHTS UNTIL THE SNOW DEMONS HAVE MERCY AND UNLEASH A BLIZZARD.
SNOW, SNOW! HIGH AND LOW! WHEREVER WE GO! LET IT BLOW! TO AND FRO! HI-DE-HO! SNOW! SNOW! SNOW!
WELL, I'LL COME OUT IN EARLY JANUARY AND SEE HOW YOU'RE DOING.
TELL MOM I'LL NEED MY MEALS OUT HERE AND I WON'T BE GOING TO SCHOOL TOMORROW.

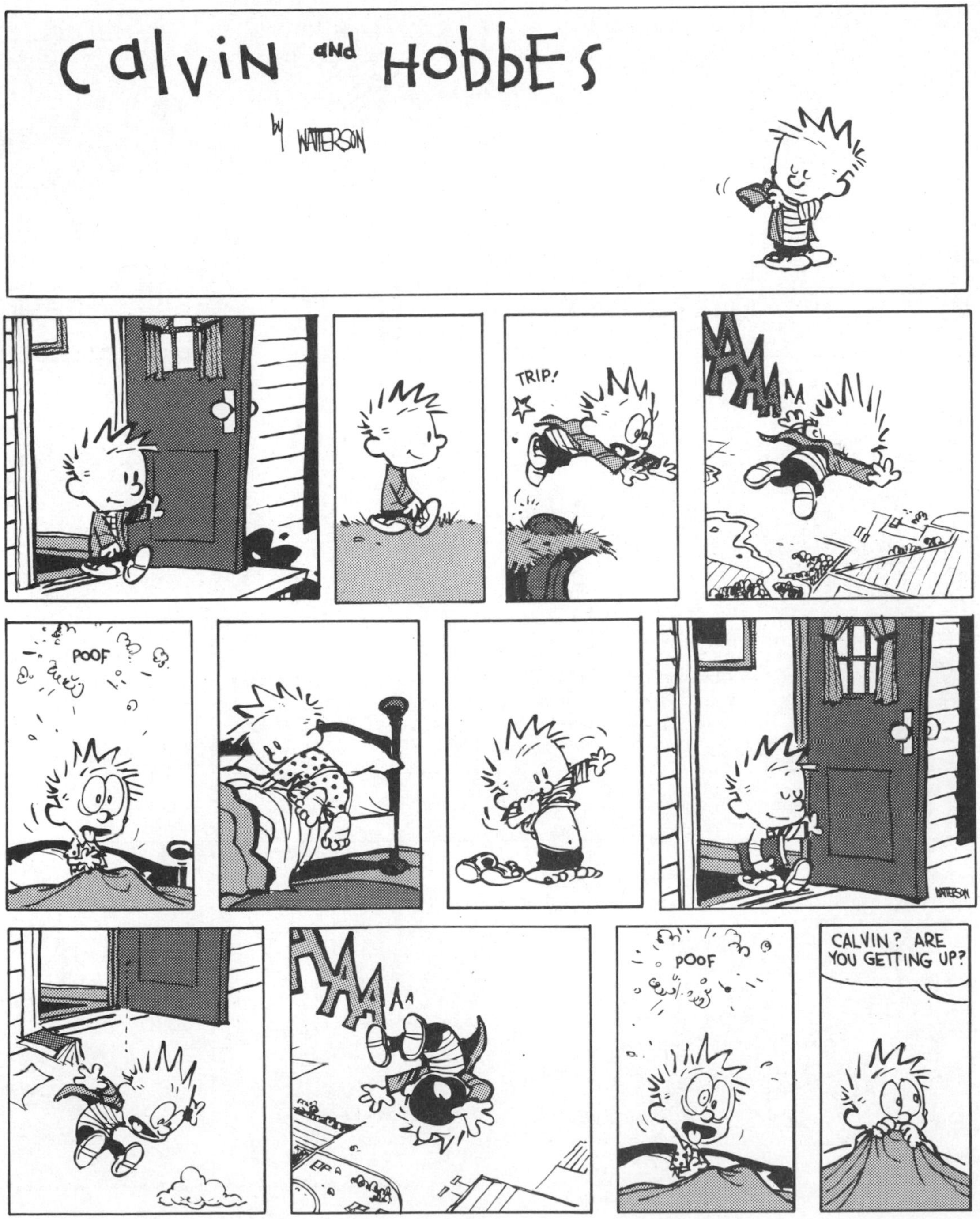
Calvin and HOBBES
by WATTERSON
TRIP!
AAAAAA
POOF
WATTERSON
AAAAA
POOF
CALVIN? ARE YOU GETTING UP?

MOM AND DAD WON'T BE TOO HAPPY ABOUT **THIS**. NO SIR.

DAD WILL HAVE TO BOLT MY BED TO THE CEILING TONIGHT, AND MOM WILL HAVE TO STAND ON A STEPLADDER TO HAND ME DINNER.

THEN I'LL HAVE TO HOLD MY PLATE UPSIDE-DOWN ABOVE MY HEAD AND SCRAPE THE FOOD OFF THE UNDERSIDE! AND IF I SPILL ANYTHING, IT WILL FLY 10 FEET UP TO THE FLOOR AND SPLOT!

THIS IS GOING TO BE THE MOST FUN I'VE EVER HAD!

ALL THIS WIDE OPEN CEILING SPACE! I WISH I COULD GET MY ROLLER SKATES.

HEY, MAYBE I CAN CLIMB UP THIS BOOKCASE AND WHEN I GET TO THE BOTTOM SHELF, LEAP TO A CHAIR!

THEN I CAN PULL MYSELF ACROSS TO OTHER PIECES OF FURNITURE AND WORK MY WAY TO MY TOY CHEST.

...I CAN HEAR MOM NOW: "HOW ON EARTH DID YOU GET SNEAKER PRINTS ON THE UNDERSIDE OF EACH SHELF?!"

THERE! I THINK I CAN JUMP TO THAT CHAIR AND HANG ONTO THE BACK.

GEERONIMOOO!

¡WHOAA!

WHAM!

GREAT. JUST GREAT.

CALVIN, QUIT BANGING AROUND!

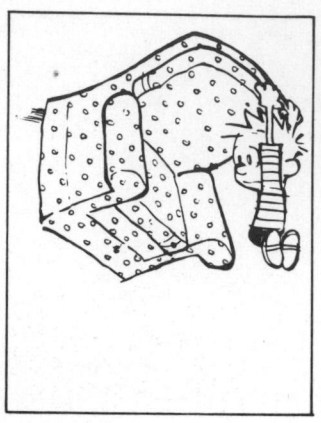

RRG!
MMF!

GETTING ANY *HOMEWORK* DONE, OR ARE YOU JUST RUINING FURNITURE?

MAYBE I'M HANGING HERE FOR DEAR *LIFE!* EVER THINK OF *THAT?*

I'M *TELLING* YOU, MY PERSONAL GRAVITY REVERSED ITS POLARITY! I FALL *UP* NOW!

I'VE BEEN TRAPPED ON THE CEILING! I COULDN'T DO MY HOMEWORK UP *THERE!* MY DESK IS ON THE *FLOOR!*

YOU SHOULD BE GLAD I WASN'T *OUTSIDE* WHEN IT HAPPENED, OR I'D BE SAILING THROUGH THE IONOSPHERE!

RIGHT. NOW I DON'T WANT TO HEAR ANY MORE NONSENSE UNTIL YOU'RE THROUGH WITH YOUR HOMEWORK, UNDERSTAND?

DON'T LET GO! DON'T LET GO!

IT'S... IT'S A MIRACLE! MY PERSONAL GRAVITY IS BACK TO NORMAL!

GLAD TO HEAR IT. NOW DO YOUR MATH.

YOU BET, MOM. BOY, WHAT A RELIEF TO BE PULLED DOWN INSTEAD OF UP!

I'LL CHECK YOUR PROGRESS IN A LITTLE BIT.

UH OH.

34

WELL? HOW'S YOUR MATH COMING ALONG?

I'VE ALMOST STARTED!

OH BROTHER! ANOTHER "DISCUSSION" ABOUT MY STUDY HABITS AND THE IMPORTANCE OF HOMEWORK.

I TRIED EXPLAINING THAT IT'S HARD TO STUDY WHEN ONE'S SIZE SUDDENLY STARTS INCREASING, BUT DOES *SHE* CARE?! HAH!

NO, IT'S JUST BLAH BLAH BLAH, LIKE IT'S ALL *MY* FAULT! MOM'S NEVER BEEN AS BIG AS A GALAXY, SO SHE CAN'T UNDERSTAND HOW ANYONE *ELSE* COULD BE! SHEEESH.

OOPS, IT LOOKS LIKE SHE'S WRAPPING UP. BETTER START NODDING.

GOOD. I'M GLAD WE HAD THIS LITTLE TALK.

DOING HOMEWORK?

YEAHHHH... BOY, YOU MISSED THE SHOW.

I GOT A BIG LECTURE FROM MOM JUST BECAUSE I GOT STUCK ON THE CEILING AND THEN GREW SO BIG I FELL OFF THE PLANET WHEN I WAS SUPPOSED TO BE DOING MY MATH!

GEE, *THAT'S* NOT VERY FAIR.

YOU SAID IT. HERE, HOW ABOUT HELPING ME HURRY UP WITH THESE PROBLEMS?

SURE! TIGERS ARE GREAT AT MATH! NOW WHAT DO THESE LITTLE HORIZONTAL LINES MEAN?

THAT'S A MINUS SIGN. LET ME KNOW WHEN YOU'RE DONE, OK? I'LL BE READING COMIC BOOKS.

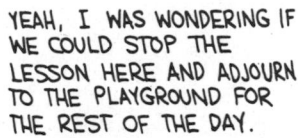

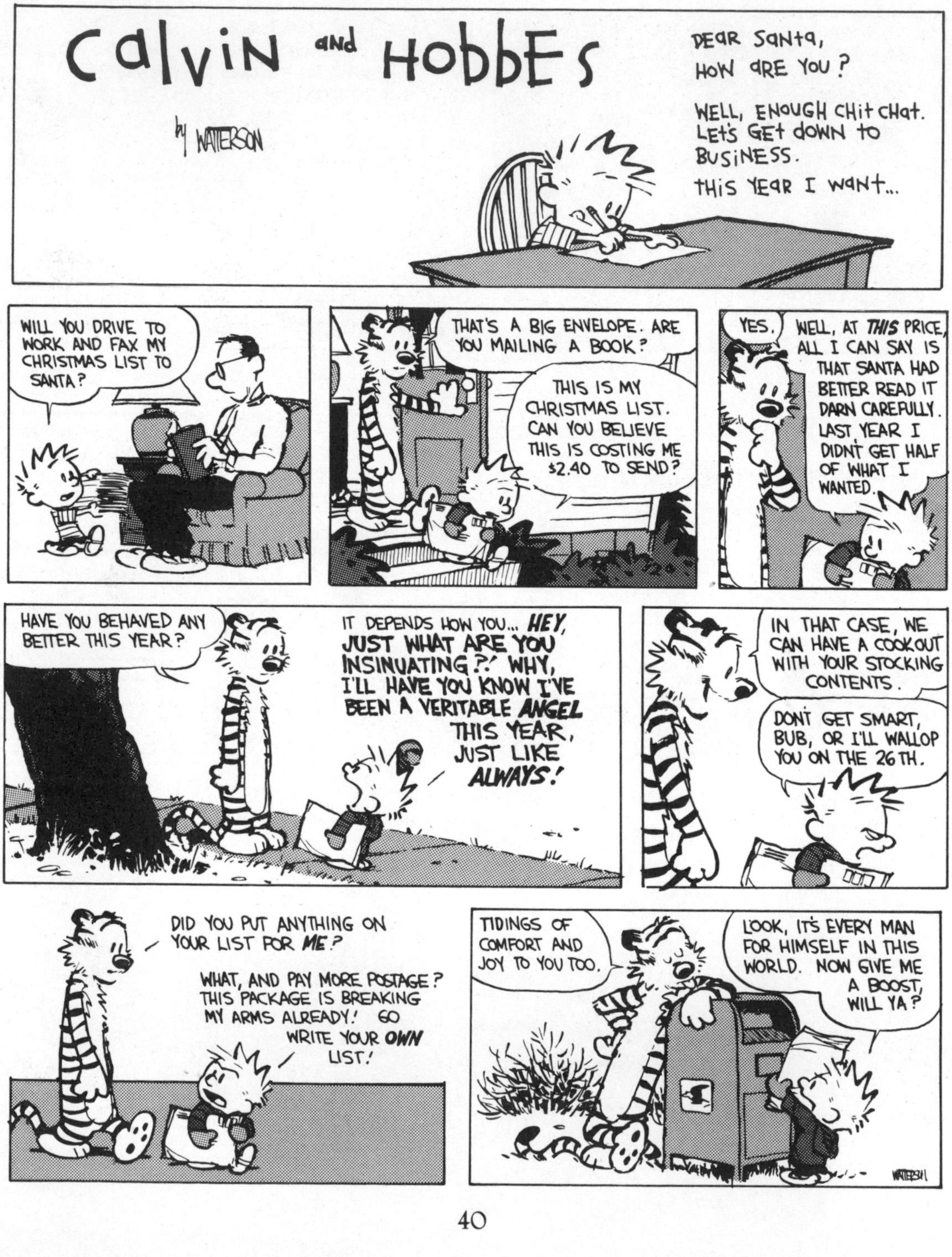
Calvin and HOBBES
by WATTERSON
DEAR SANTA, HOW ARE YOU?
WELL, ENOUGH CHIT CHAT. LET'S GET DOWN TO BUSINESS.
THIS YEAR I WANT...
WILL YOU DRIVE TO WORK AND FAX MY CHRISTMAS LIST TO SANTA?
THAT'S A BIG ENVELOPE. ARE YOU MAILING A BOOK?
THIS IS MY CHRISTMAS LIST. CAN YOU BELIEVE THIS IS COSTING ME $2.40 TO SEND?
YES.
WELL, AT THIS PRICE, ALL I CAN SAY IS THAT SANTA HAD BETTER READ IT DARN CAREFULLY. LAST YEAR I DIDN'T GET HALF OF WHAT I WANTED.
HAVE YOU BEHAVED ANY BETTER THIS YEAR?
IT DEPENDS HOW YOU... HEY, JUST WHAT ARE YOU INSINUATING?! WHY, I'LL HAVE YOU KNOW I'VE BEEN A VERITABLE ANGEL THIS YEAR, JUST LIKE ALWAYS!
IN THAT CASE, WE CAN HAVE A COOKOUT WITH YOUR STOCKING CONTENTS.
DON'T GET SMART, BUB, OR I'LL WALLOP YOU ON THE 26TH.
DID YOU PUT ANYTHING ON YOUR LIST FOR ME?
WHAT, AND PAY MORE POSTAGE? THIS PACKAGE IS BREAKING MY ARMS ALREADY! GO WRITE YOUR OWN LIST!
TIDINGS OF COMFORT AND JOY TO YOU TOO.
LOOK, IT'S EVERY MAN FOR HIMSELF IN THIS WORLD. NOW GIVE ME A BOOST, WILL YA?
WATTERSON

ARE THERE ANY MONSTERS UNDER MY BED TONIGHT?

OF COURSE NOT. COME UNDER AND SEE FOR YOURSELF.

YEAH, COME AND SEE. HEH HEH HEH.

OH RIGHT! YOU THINK I'M FALLING FOR *THAT*?! WHO AM I *TALKING* TO IF THERE AREN'T ANY MONSTERS DOWN THERE?!

UMM.. UH..

THEY'RE ALL TEETH AND DIGESTIVE TRACT. NO BRAINS AT ALL.

WHY, WE'RE DUST BALLS!

YEAH, *LITTLE* DUST BALLS!

EWW! WHAT'S *THIS* DISGUSTING STUFF?!

IT'S SPIDER PIE. YOU CAN PICK OUT THE BIG LEGS AND GIVE THEM TO YOUR DAD IF THEY'RE TOO HAIRY FOR YOU.

S-S-SPIDER P-PIE?

WHY, I BELIEVE WE'RE GOING TO HAVE A QUIET DINNER FOR ONCE.

I KNOW *I* DON'T FEEL LIKE OPENING MY MOUTH.

HEY, I *LIKE* IT!

WANT TO GO PLAY OUTSIDE?

NO, IT'S TOO MUCH TROUBLE. *FIRST* I'D HAVE TO GET UP. *THEN* I'D HAVE TO PUT ON A COAT. *THEN* I'D HAVE TO FIND MY HAT AND PUT *IT* ON. (SIGH) THEN WE'D RUN AROUND AND I'D GET TIRED, AND WHEN WE CAME IN I'D HAVE TO TAKE ALL THAT STUFF *OFF*. NO WAY.

SO WHAT ARE YOU GOING TO DO INSTEAD?

I'M JUST GOING TO SIT HERE AND WAIT FOR A GOOD TV SHOW TO COME ON.

I'LL TELL YOUR MOM TO TURN YOU TOWARD THE LIGHT AND WATER YOU PERIODICALLY.

INSTEAD OF MAKING SMART REMARKS, YOU COULD GET ME THE REMOTE CONTROL.

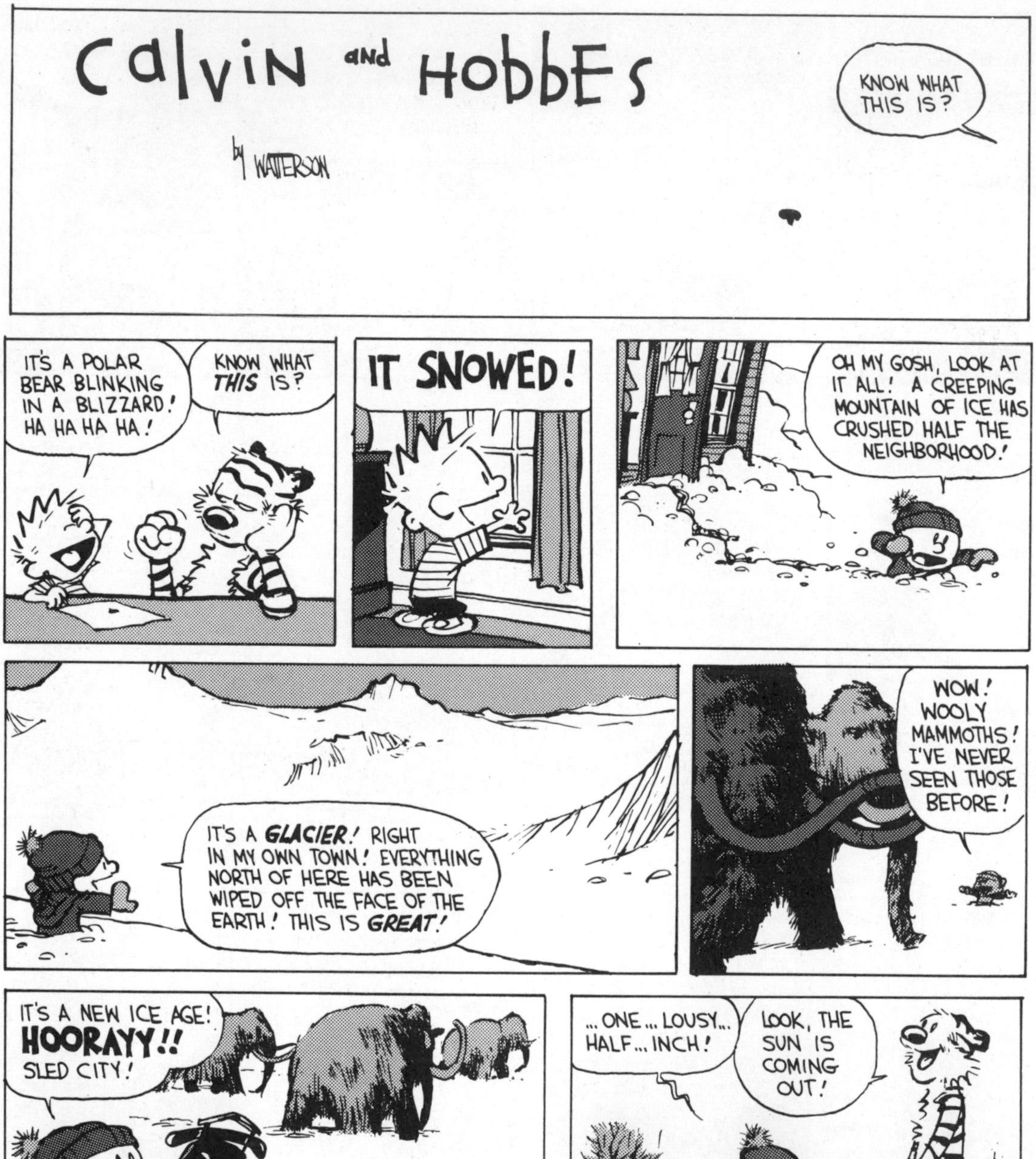
Calvin and HOBBES
by WATTERSON
KNOW WHAT THIS IS?
IT'S A POLAR BEAR BLINKING IN A BLIZZARD! HA HA HA HA!
KNOW WHAT THIS IS?
IT SNOWED!
OH MY GOSH, LOOK AT IT ALL! A CREEPING MOUNTAIN OF ICE HAS CRUSHED HALF THE NEIGHBORHOOD!
IT'S A GLACIER! RIGHT IN MY OWN TOWN! EVERYTHING NORTH OF HERE HAS BEEN WIPED OFF THE FACE OF THE EARTH! THIS IS GREAT!
WOW! WOOLY MAMMOTHS! I'VE NEVER SEEN THOSE BEFORE!
IT'S A NEW ICE AGE! HOORAYY!! SLED CITY!
LOOK, THE SUN IS COMING OUT!
...ONE... LOUSY... HALF... INCH!
WATTERSON

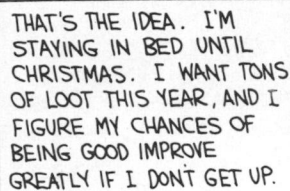

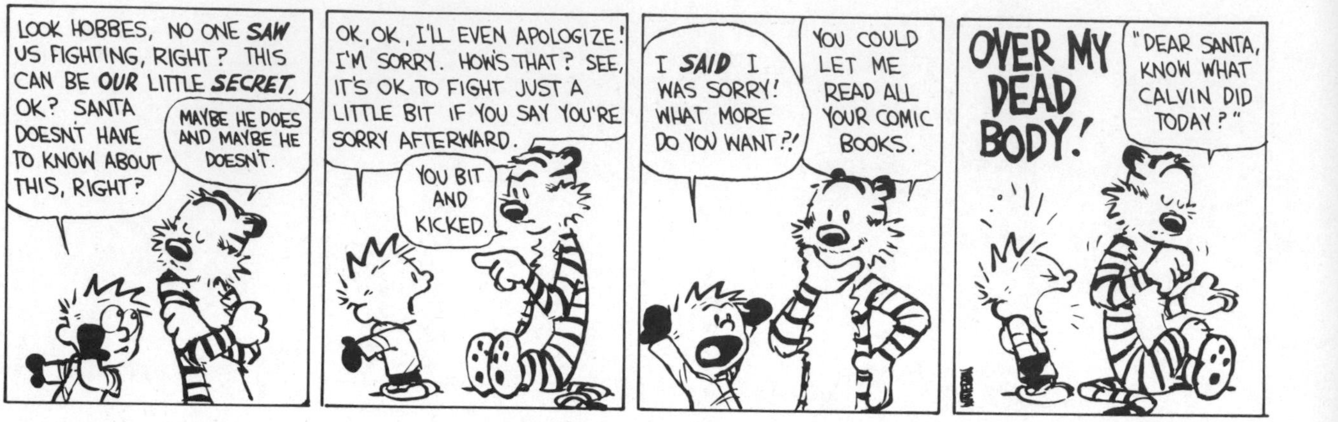
LOOK HOBBES, NO ONE SAW US FIGHTING, RIGHT? THIS CAN BE OUR LITTLE SECRET, OK? SANTA DOESN'T HAVE TO KNOW ABOUT THIS, RIGHT?
MAYBE HE DOES AND MAYBE HE DOESN'T.
OK, OK, I'LL EVEN APOLOGIZE! I'M SORRY. HOW'S THAT? SEE, IT'S OK TO FIGHT JUST A LITTLE BIT IF YOU SAY YOU'RE SORRY AFTERWARD.
YOU BIT AND KICKED.
I SAID I WAS SORRY! WHAT MORE DO YOU WANT?!
YOU COULD LET ME READ ALL YOUR COMIC BOOKS.
OVER MY DEAD BODY!
"DEAR SANTA, KNOW WHAT CALVIN DID TODAY?"

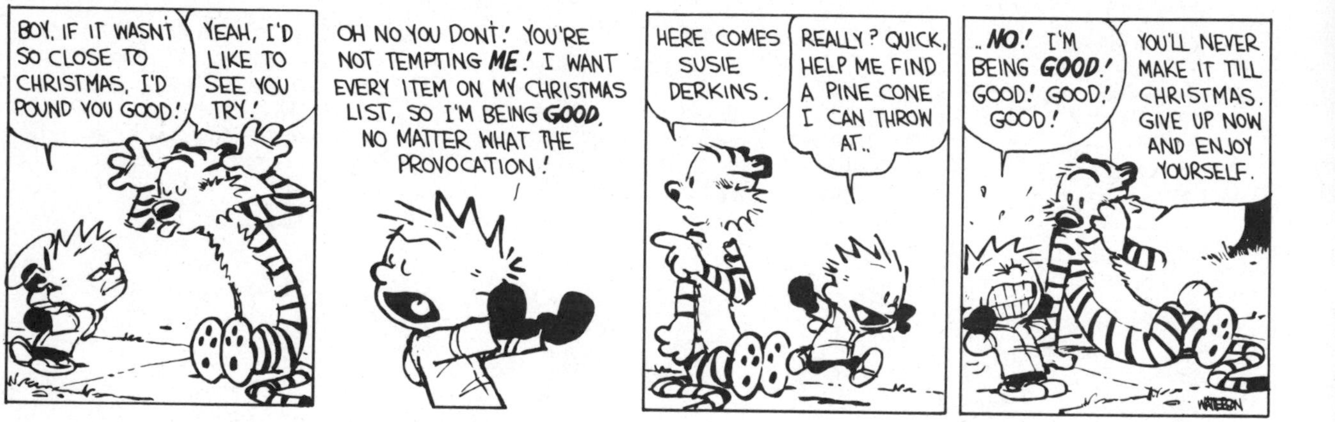
BOY, IF IT WASN'T SO CLOSE TO CHRISTMAS, I'D POUND YOU GOOD!
YEAH, I'D LIKE TO SEE YOU TRY!
OH NO YOU DON'T! YOU'RE NOT TEMPTING ME! I WANT EVERY ITEM ON MY CHRISTMAS LIST, SO I'M BEING GOOD, NO MATTER WHAT THE PROVOCATION!
HERE COMES SUSIE DERKINS.
REALLY? QUICK, HELP ME FIND A PINE CONE I CAN THROW AT..
..NO! I'M BEING GOOD! GOOD! GOOD! GOOD!
YOU'LL NEVER MAKE IT TILL CHRISTMAS. GIVE UP NOW AND ENJOY YOURSELF.

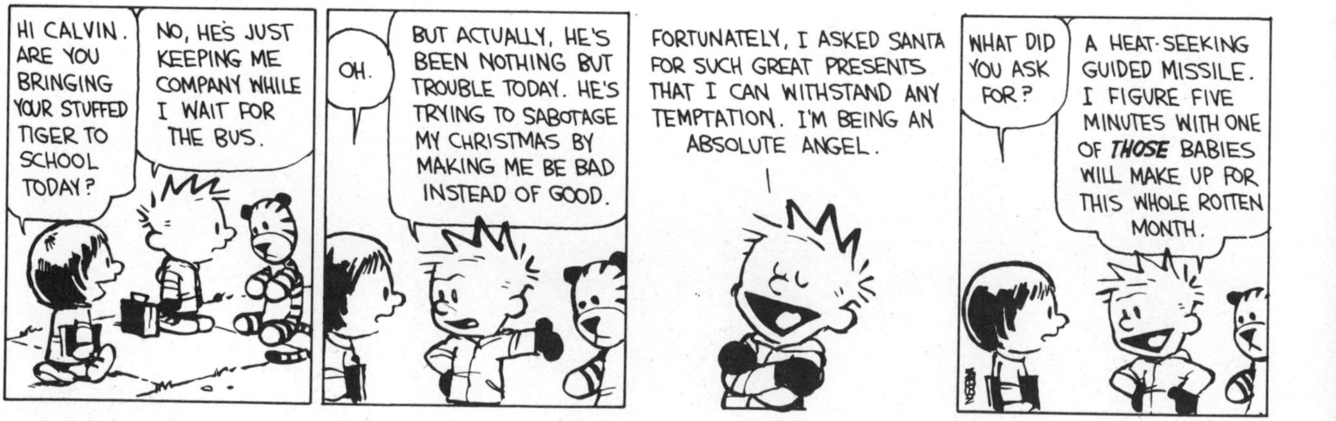
HI CALVIN. ARE YOU BRINGING YOUR STUFFED TIGER TO SCHOOL TODAY?
NO, HE'S JUST KEEPING ME COMPANY WHILE I WAIT FOR THE BUS.
OH.
BUT ACTUALLY, HE'S BEEN NOTHING BUT TROUBLE TODAY. HE'S TRYING TO SABOTAGE MY CHRISTMAS BY MAKING ME BE BAD INSTEAD OF GOOD.
FORTUNATELY, I ASKED SANTA FOR SUCH GREAT PRESENTS THAT I CAN WITHSTAND ANY TEMPTATION. I'M BEING AN ABSOLUTE ANGEL.
WHAT DID YOU ASK FOR?
A HEAT-SEEKING GUIDED MISSILE. I FIGURE FIVE MINUTES WITH ONE OF THOSE BABIES WILL MAKE UP FOR THIS WHOLE ROTTEN MONTH.

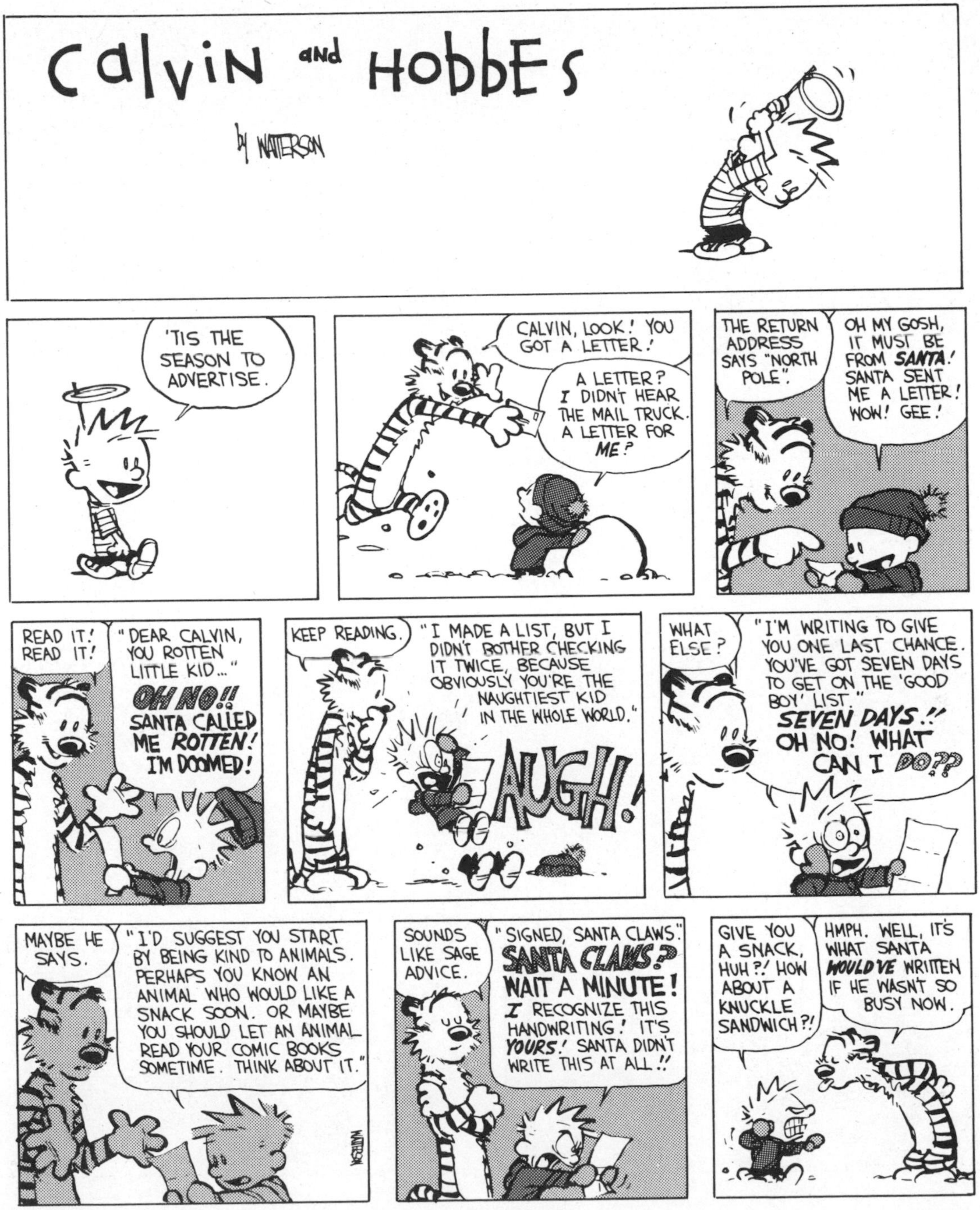
Calvin and HOBBES
by WATTERSON
'TIS THE SEASON TO ADVERTISE.
CALVIN, LOOK! YOU GOT A LETTER!
A LETTER? I DIDN'T HEAR THE MAIL TRUCK. A LETTER FOR ME?
THE RETURN ADDRESS SAYS "NORTH POLE".
OH MY GOSH, IT MUST BE FROM SANTA! SANTA SENT ME A LETTER! WOW! GEE!
READ IT! READ IT!
"DEAR CALVIN, YOU ROTTEN LITTLE KID..."
OH NO!! SANTA CALLED ME ROTTEN! I'M DOOMED!
KEEP READING.
"I MADE A LIST, BUT I DIDN'T BOTHER CHECKING IT TWICE, BECAUSE OBVIOUSLY YOU'RE THE NAUGHTIEST KID IN THE WHOLE WORLD."
AUGH!
WHAT ELSE?
"I'M WRITING TO GIVE YOU ONE LAST CHANCE. YOU'VE GOT SEVEN DAYS TO GET ON THE 'GOOD BOY' LIST."
SEVEN DAYS!? OH NO! WHAT CAN I DO??
MAYBE HE SAYS.
"I'D SUGGEST YOU START BY BEING KIND TO ANIMALS. PERHAPS YOU KNOW AN ANIMAL WHO WOULD LIKE A SNACK SOON. OR MAYBE YOU SHOULD LET AN ANIMAL READ YOUR COMIC BOOKS SOMETIME. THINK ABOUT IT."
SOUNDS LIKE SAGE ADVICE.
"SIGNED, SANTA CLAWS."
SANTA CLAWS? WAIT A MINUTE! I RECOGNIZE THIS HANDWRITING! IT'S YOURS! SANTA DIDN'T WRITE THIS AT ALL!!
GIVE YOU A SNACK, HUH?! HOW ABOUT A KNUCKLE SANDWICH?!
HMPH. WELL, IT'S WHAT SANTA WOULD'VE WRITTEN IF HE WASN'T SO BUSY NOW.

WANT TO HELP ME WRITE A BOOK?

SURE. WHAT'S IT ABOUT?

WELL, YOU KNOW WHAT HISTORICAL FICTION IS? THIS IS SORT OF LIKE THAT. I'M WRITING A FICTIONAL AUTOBIOGRAPHY.

IT'S THE STORY OF MY LIFE, BUT WITH A LOT OF PARTS COMPLETELY MADE UP.

WHY WOULD YOU MAKE UP YOUR OWN LIFE?

BECAUSE IN MY BOOK I HAVE A FLAME THROWER!

STILL AND QUIET FELINE FORM, IN THE SUN, ASLEEP AND WARM. HIS TAIL IS LIMP, HIS WHISKERS DROOPED. MAN, WHAT COULD MAKE THIS CAT SO POOPED?

SHEESHH..

HI MOM! I'M MAKING MY OWN NEWSPAPER TO REPORT THE EVENTS OF OUR HOUSEHOLD.

THAT'S NICE.

NOW I'M LOOKING FOR A PAGE ONE LEAD STORY. CAN I INTERVIEW YOU?

SURE.

OK, WHAT ARE YOU CUTTING UP THERE FOR DINNER?

FISH.

KNIFE WIELDING MOTHER HACKS ICHTHYOID! GRIM MELEE IS EVENING RITUAL! SUBURBAN FAMILY DEVOURS VICTIM!

OUT OF THE KITCHEN! OUT! OUT!

Christmas Eve

ON WINDOW PANES, THE ICY FROST
LEAVES FEATHERED PATTERNS, CRISSED & CROSSED,
BUT IN OUR HOUSE THE CHRISTMAS TREE
IS DECORATED FESTIVELY
WITH TINY DOTS OF COLORED LIGHT
THAT COZY UP THIS WINTER NIGHT.
CHRISTMAS SONGS, FAMILIAR, SLOW,
PLAY SOFTLY ON THE RADIO.
POPS AND HISSES FROM THE FIRE
WHISTLE WITH THE BELLS AND CHOIR.
MY TIGER IS NOW FAST ASLEEP
ON HIS BACK AND DREAMING DEEP.
WHEN THE FIRE MAKES HIM HOT,
HE TURNS TO WARM WHATEVER'S NOT.
PROPPED AGAINST HIM ON THE RUG,
I GIVE MY FRIEND A GENTLE HUG.
TOMORROW'S WHAT I'M WAITING FOR,
BUT I CAN WAIT A LITTLE MORE.

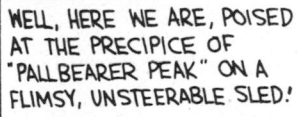

I SEE YOU, HOBBES! MAN, WHAT A LOUSY SHOT! TIGERS CAN'T THROW WORTH A..

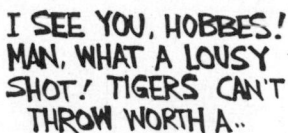

SMACK!

I JUST THREW THE FIRST ONE SO YOU'D TURN AROUND.

A NEW DECADE IS COMING UP.

YEAH, BIG DEAL! HMPH.

WHERE ARE THE FLYING CARS? WHERE ARE THE MOON COLONIES? WHERE ARE THE PERSONAL ROBOTS AND THE ZERO GRAVITY BOOTS, HUH? YOU CALL THIS A NEW DECADE?! YOU CALL THIS THE FUTURE?? *HA!*

WHERE ARE THE ROCKET PACKS? WHERE ARE THE DISINTEGRATION RAYS? WHERE ARE THE FLOATING CITIES?

FRANKLY, I'M NOT SURE PEOPLE HAVE THE BRAINS TO MANAGE THE TECHNOLOGY THEY'VE *GOT.*

I MEAN, *LOOK* AT THIS! WE STILL HAVE *WEATHER?!* GIVE ME A BREAK!

FOR YOUR INFORMATION, I'M **STAYING** LIKE THIS, AND EVERYONE ELSE CAN JUST GET **USED** TO IT! IF PEOPLE DON'T LIKE ME THE WAY I AM, WELL, **TOUGH** BEANS! IT'S A FREE COUNTRY! I DON'T NEED ANYONE'S PERMISSION TO BE THE WAY I WANT! THIS IS HOW I AM - TAKE IT OR LEAVE IT!

BEFORE GOING DOWN A STEEP HILL LIKE THIS, ONE SHOULD ALWAYS GIVE HIS SLED A SAFETY CHECK.

RIGHT.

SEAT BELTS?

NONE.

SIGNALS?

NONE.

BRAKES?

NONE.

STEERING?

NONE.

WHEEEEEE

HOW COLD IS IT OUTSIDE?

I DON'T KNOW. WHY DON'T YOU CHECK?

IT'S PRETTY DARN COLD, I'D SAY.

LET ME SHOW YOU AN INTERESTING GADGET THAT'S HANGING OUTSIDE THE WINDOW.

THIS IS THE PART OF WINTER I LIKE BEST... WHEN YOU COME INSIDE, FREEZING COLD AND SOAKED...

...AND YOU PUT ON FRESH DRY CLOTHES, AND RUN UP TO THE WARM KITCHEN, WHERE MOM'S GOT A STEAMING MUG OF HOT CHOCOLATE WAITING FOR YOU!

MOM?... MOM?? HEY MOM!

"CALVIN, I'M NEXT DOOR. DON'T HAVE ANYTHING TO EAT, OR YOU'LL SPOIL YOUR APPETITE. MOM."

IT'S GOING TO BE A LONG, COLD, DARK WINTER.

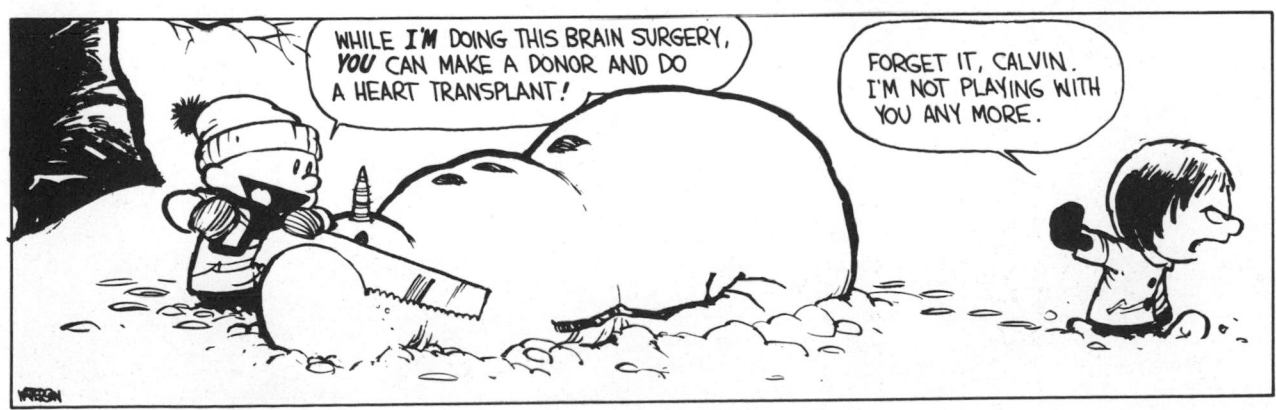

WHILE *I'M* DOING THIS BRAIN SURGERY, *YOU* CAN MAKE A DONOR AND DO A HEART TRANSPLANT!

FORGET IT, CALVIN. I'M NOT PLAYING WITH YOU ANY MORE.

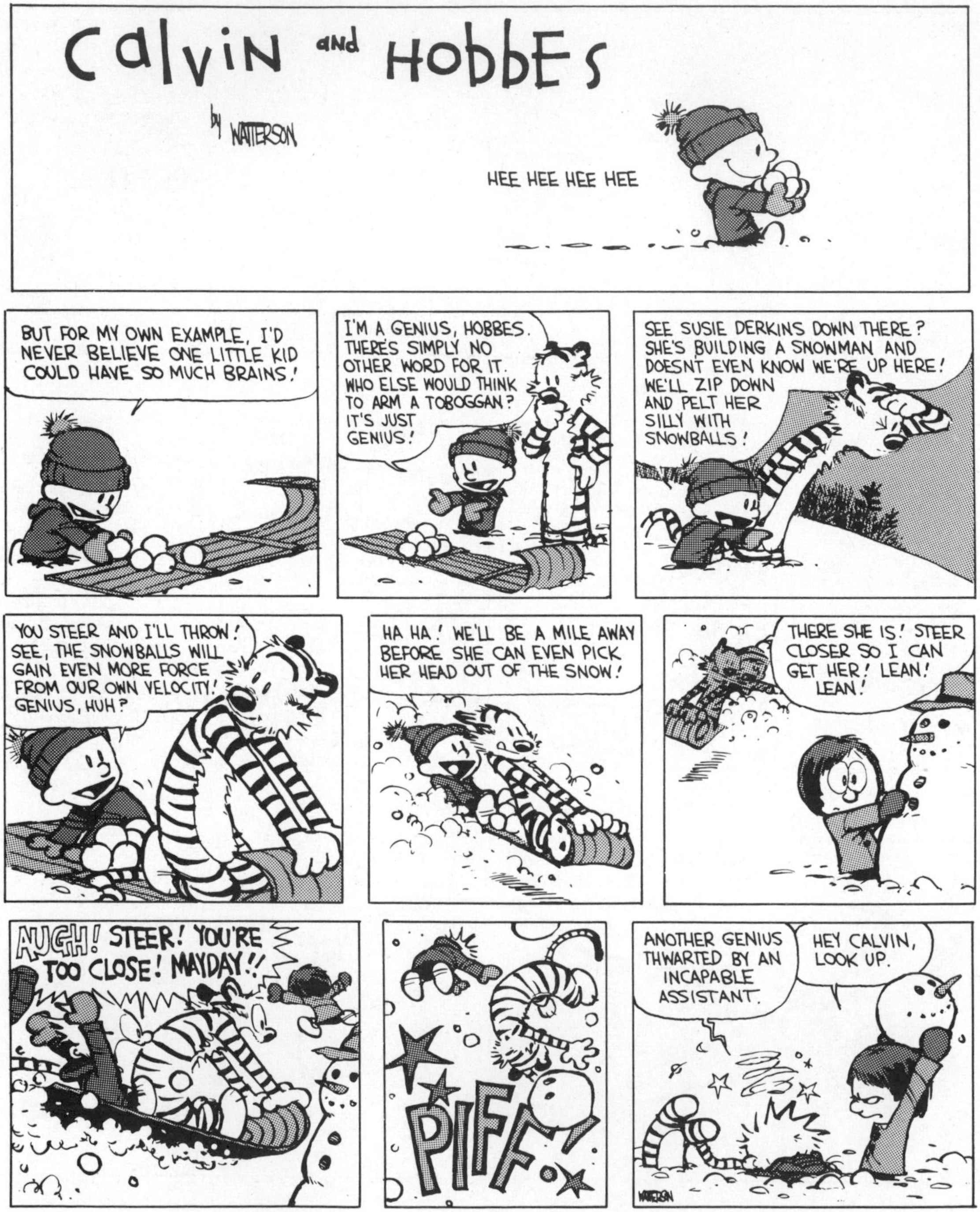

Calvin and HOBBES
by WATTERSON
HEE HEE HEE HEE
BUT FOR MY OWN EXAMPLE, I'D NEVER BELIEVE ONE LITTLE KID COULD HAVE SO MUCH BRAINS!
I'M A GENIUS, HOBBES. THERE'S SIMPLY NO OTHER WORD FOR IT. WHO ELSE WOULD THINK TO ARM A TOBOGGAN? IT'S JUST GENIUS!
SEE SUSIE DERKINS DOWN THERE? SHE'S BUILDING A SNOWMAN AND DOESN'T EVEN KNOW WE'RE UP HERE! WE'LL ZIP DOWN AND PELT HER SILLY WITH SNOWBALLS!
YOU STEER AND I'LL THROW! SEE, THE SNOWBALLS WILL GAIN EVEN MORE FORCE FROM OUR OWN VELOCITY! GENIUS, HUH?
HA HA! WE'LL BE A MILE AWAY BEFORE SHE CAN EVEN PICK HER HEAD OUT OF THE SNOW!
THERE SHE IS! STEER CLOSER SO I CAN GET HER! LEAN! LEAN!
AUGH! STEER! YOU'RE TOO CLOSE! MAYDAY!!
PIFF
ANOTHER GENIUS THWARTED BY AN INCAPABLE ASSISTANT.
HEY CALVIN, LOOK UP.
WATTERSON

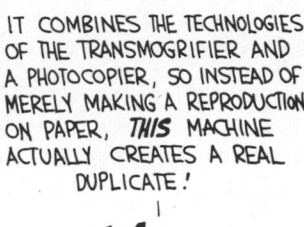

THE DUPLICATOR WORKED! HOBBES, MEET MY DUPLICATE!

HEY, NICE ROOM.

OOG, I'M NOT SURE I'M READY FOR THIS.

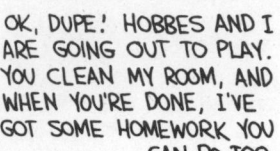

OK, DUPE! HOBBES AND I ARE GOING OUT TO PLAY. YOU CLEAN MY ROOM, AND WHEN YOU'RE DONE, I'VE GOT SOME HOMEWORK YOU CAN DO, TOO.

WHAT?!

FORGET IT, BUB! FIND SOME OTHER SUCKER TO DO YOUR DIRTY WORK! LAST ONE OUTSIDE IS A ROTTEN EGG!

HEY! COME BACK HERE!

HE'S A DUPLICATE OF YOU, ALL RIGHT.

WHAT DO YOU MEAN? THIS GUY IS A TOTAL JERK!

WHERE ARE YOU GOING? DID YOU CLEAN YOUR ROOM LIKE I ASKED YOU TO?

I'M GOING OUTSIDE. CALVIN CAN CLEAN HIS OWN ROOM.

I DON'T WANT ANY NONSENSE, CALVIN. GO UPSTAIRS.

CALVIN? I'M NOT CALVIN. I'M HIS DUPLICATE. CALVIN'S IN HIS ROOM.

WHAT DID I JUST SAY? NO NONSENSE, CALVIN! GO CLEAN YOUR ROOM.

BOY, YOU ARE A CRABBY LADY! WHO ARE YOU? CALVIN'S CRUEL GOVERNESS?

THAT DOES IT.

C'MON, HOBBES. WE'D BETTER GO FIND MY DUPLICATE BEFORE HE GETS ME IN TROUBLE.

I'M TELLING YOU, LADY, YOU'VE GOT THE WRONG GUY! I'M A DUPLICATE OF CALVIN! CALVIN'S IN HIS ROOM!

WE'LL SEE ABOUT THAT. GIVE ME YOUR COAT.

SEE, CALVIN? THERE'S NO ONE HERE. NOW THAT'S ENOUGH GAMES. CLEAN YOUR ROOM, OK?

CALVIN?

I DON'T SEE HIM, HOBBES. MAYBE HE'S OUTSIDE, HUH?

WE'D BETTER HURRY. I THINK I HEAR YOUR MOM COMING DOWN THE STAIRS.

OK DUPLICATES, LISTEN UP. AS LONG AS YOU'RE ALL HERE AND I DON'T KNOW HOW TO GET RID OF YOU, WE MIGHT AS WELL COOPERATE.

SPECIFICALLY, WITH FIVE DUPLICATES, WE CAN DIVIDE UP THE SCHOOL WEEK SO THERE'S ONE DUPLICATE FOR EACH DAY.

IF THE REST OF US LAY LOW, WE CAN TAKE TURNS GOING TO SCHOOL, AND NO ONE WILL BE THE WISER!

GREAT!

NOW THAT STILL LEAVES US WITH THE QUESTION OF WHO GETS THE BED TONIGHT.

WE'LL FIGHT YOU FOR IT.

HI CALVIN.

I'M NOT CALVIN. I'M DUPLICATE NUMBER TWO.

WHAT ARE YOU TALKING ABOUT?

WE DREW STRAWS, AND TODAY'S MY DAY TO GO TO SCHOOL. WE'RE ALL TAKING TURNS SO WE EACH ONLY GO ONCE A WEEK.

CALVIN, YOU ARE SO WEIRD I'M NOT EVEN GOING TO TALK TO YOU.

I'M NOT CALVIN.

I WISH I LIVED SOMEPLACE WHERE I WENT TO A NORMAL BUS STOP.

ARE YOU IN CALVIN'S CLASS? WILL YOU HELP ME FIND HIS LOCKER?

CALVIN, WOULD YOU PLEASE DEMONSTRATE THE HOMEWORK PROBLEM YOU WERE ASSIGNED YESTERDAY?

I WASN'T HERE YESTERDAY.

YES, YOU WERE, CALVIN. DIDN'T YOU DO YOUR PROBLEM?

I'M NOT CALVIN. I'M DUPLICATE NUMBER FIVE. DUPLICATE *TWO* WAS HERE YESTERDAY, NOT *ME*. WE'RE ALL TAKING TURNS. NUMBER TWO WILL BE BACK NEXT WEEK, AND YOU CAN ASK HIM TO DO THE PROBLEM *THEN*.

LOOK, I DON'T SEE WHAT'S SO HARD ABOUT THIS!

PRINCIPAL

QUIZ:
Jack and Joe leave their homes at the same time and drive toward each other. Jack drives at 60 mph, while Joe drives at 30 mph. They pass each other in 10 minutes.

How far apart were Jack and Joe when they started?

IT WAS ANOTHER BAFFLING CASE. BUT THEN, YOU DON'T HIRE A **PRIVATE EYE** FOR THE **EASY** ONES...

I'D PLANNED TO TAKE THE DAY **OFF** AND SPEND TIME WITH A COUPLE OF **BUDDIES**. MY BUDDIES TRAVEL LIGHT AND THEY'RE FUN TO HAVE AROUND. ONE TRAVELS IN A HOLSTER, AND THE OTHER IN A HIP FLASK.

MY NAME IS **BULLET**. TRACER BULLET. WHAT PEOPLE **CALL** ME IS SOMETHING ELSE AGAIN. I'M A PRIVATE EYE. IT SAYS SO ON MY DOOR.

THE **LAST** THING I WANTED THIS MORNING WAS A **CASE** TO SOLVE, BUT THE DAME WHO BROUGHT IT WAS **PERSUASIVE**. MOST DAMES **ARE**, SOMEHOW.

GET TO WORK, CALVIN.

I TOLD HER IT WOULD COST HER FIFTY GREENBACKS A DAY, PLUS EXPENSES.

I STEPPED OUT INTO THE RAINY STREETS AND REVIEWED THE FACTS. THERE WEREN'T MANY.

TWO SAPS, JACK AND JOE, DRIVE TOWARD EACH OTHER AT 60 AND 30 MPH. AFTER 10 MINUTES, THEY PASS. I'M SUPPOSED TO FIND OUT HOW FAR APART THEY STARTED.

QUESTIONS POUR DOWN LIKE THE RAIN. WHO **ARE** THESE MUGS? WHAT WERE THEY TRYING TO ACCOMPLISH? WHY WAS JACK IN SUCH A HURRY? AND WHAT DIFFERENCE DOES IT MAKE WHERE THEY STARTED FROM??

I HAD A HUNCH THAT, BEFORE THIS WAS OVER, I'D BE SORRY I ASKED.

FIRST I FIGURED I'D TRY THE DERKINS DAME. SUSIE AND I NEVER HIT IT OFF, ALTHOUGH OCCASIONALLY WE HIT EACH OTHER.

SUSIE HAD A FACE THAT SUGGESTED SOMEBODY UPSTAIRS HAD A WEIRD SENSE OF HUMOR, BUT I WASN'T GOING TO HER PLACE FOR LAUGHS. I NEEDED INFORMATION.

THE WAY *I* LOOKED AT IT, DERKINS ACTED AWFULLY SMUG FOR A DAME WHO HAD A HEAD FOR NUMBERS AND NOT MUCH ELSE. MAYBE SHE'S GOT SOMETHING ON JACK AND JOE. THE QUESTION IS, WILL SHE SING?

NO, I WON'T TELL YOU WHAT THE ANSWER IS! DO YOUR *OWN* WORK!

THE DERKINS DAME WASN'T TALKING. SOMEONE HAD GOTTEN TO HER FIRST AND SHUT HER UP GOOD. I KNEW SUSIE, AND CLOSING HER MOUTH WOULD'VE TAKEN SOME WORK.

I NEEDED A CLUE AND A DRINK. ONE OF THEM I KNEW WHERE TO FIND.

YOU'VE MADE ENOUGH TRIPS TO THE WATER FOUNTAIN. FINISH YOUR QUIZ.

SUDDENLY A GORILLA PULLED ME IN AN ALLEY, SQUEEZED MY SPINE INTO AN ACCORDION, AND PLAYED A POLKA ON ME WITH BRASS KNUCKLES!

YOUSE AIN'T GOIN' NOWHERE, FLATFOOT.

THE INSIDE OF MY HEAD WAS EXPLODING WITH FIREWORKS. FORTUNATELY, MY LAST THOUGHT TURNED OUT THE LIGHTS WHEN IT LEFT.

WHEN I CAME TO, THE PIECES ALL FIT TOGETHER. JACK AND JOE'S LIVES WERE DEFINED BY INTEGERS. OBVIOUSLY, THEY WERE PART OF A "NUMBERS" RACKET!

BACK IN THE OFFICE, I PULLED THE FILES ON ALL THE NUMBERS *BIG* ENOUGH TO KEEP SUSIE QUIET AND WANT ME OUT OF THE PICTURE. THE ANSWER HIT ME LIKE A .44 SLUG. IT HAD TO BE THE NUMBER THEY CALLED "MR. BILLION."

Answer: 1,000,000,000

CASE CLOSED!

TIME'S UP. BRING YOUR PAPERS FORWARD.

WHAT DID YOU GET, CALVIN? I THINK THE ANSWER'S 15.

66

CALVIN and HOBBES
by WATTERSON

I THINK THIS IS MY FAVORITE TIME OF YEAR! THE NEW SNOW MAKES EVERYTHING LOOK SO PRETTY.

WHOAAAAA! WUMPH!

I THINK THIS IS MY FAVORITE TIME OF YEAR! THE NEW SNOW MUFFLES APPROACHING FOOTSTEPS! HOO HOO!

MAN, I CAN'T WAIT FOR SPRING.

Calvin and Hobbes

by WATTERSON

LET'S HURRY DOWN THIS HILL AND GO HOME.

WHAT'S THE RUSH?

THERE'S A TV SHOW ON SLEDDING I WANT TO WATCH.

IN MY OPINION, TELEVISION VALIDATES EXISTENCE.

TAKE THIS SLED RIDE, FOR INSTANCE. THE EXPERIENCE IS FLEETING AND ELUSIVE. BY TOMORROW, WE'LL HAVE FORGOTTEN IT, AND IT MAY AS WELL HAVE NOT EVEN HAPPENED.

BUT IF WE WERE ON TV NOW, COUNTLESS VIEWERS WOULD SHARE IN THE EVENT AND CONFIRM IT! THIS RIDE WOULD BECOME A PART OF MASS CONSCIOUSNESS!

AND ON TV, THE IMPACT OF AN EVENT IS DETERMINED BY THE IMAGE, NOT ITS SUBSTANCE.

SO WITH SOME STRONG VISUALS, OUR SLED RIDE COULD CONCEIVABLY MAKE US CULTURAL *ICONS*!

INSTEAD OF BEING BORING OL' CALVIN AND HOBBES, WE'D BE "CALVIN AND HOBBES *AS SEEN ON TV*"! WOULDN'T THAT BE GREAT? DON'T YOU WISH WE WERE ON TV?

AT THIS MOMENT, I LIKE MY ANONYMITY.

I THINK WE SHOULD GO FOR THE HIGH-BROW PUBLIC TV AUDIENCE, DON'T YOU?

WATTERSON

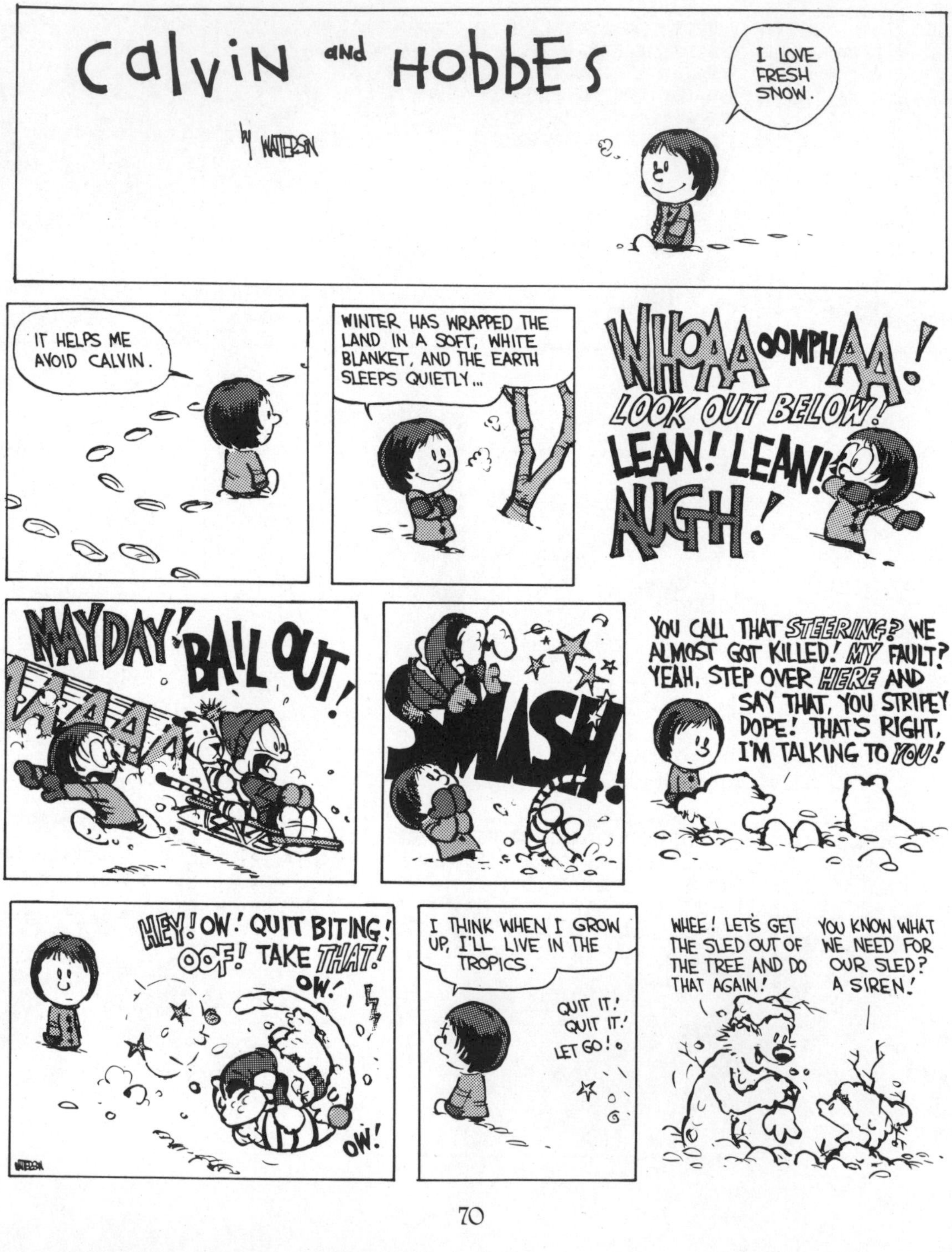
Calvin and HOBBES
by WATTERSON
I LOVE FRESH SNOW.
IT HELPS ME AVOID CALVIN.
WINTER HAS WRAPPED THE LAND IN A SOFT, WHITE BLANKET, AND THE EARTH SLEEPS QUIETLY...
WHOAA OOMPH AA!
LOOK OUT BELOW!
LEAN! LEAN!
AUGH!
MAYDAY! BAIL OUT!
WAAAA
SMASH!
YOU CALL THAT STEERING? WE ALMOST GOT KILLED! MY FAULT? YEAH, STEP OVER HERE AND SAY THAT, YOU STRIPEY DOPE! THAT'S RIGHT, I'M TALKING TO YOU!
HEY! OW! QUIT BITING! OOF! TAKE THAT!
OW!
OW!
WATTERSON
I THINK WHEN I GROW UP, I'LL LIVE IN THE TROPICS.
QUIT IT! QUIT IT! LET GO!
WHEE! LET'S GET THE SLED OUT OF THE TREE AND DO THAT AGAIN!
YOU KNOW WHAT WE NEED FOR OUR SLED? A SIREN!

W U M P !

ANY DUMB KID CAN BUILD A SNOWMAN, BUT IT TAKES A GENIUS LIKE ME TO CREATE *ART*.

THIS SNOW SCULPTURE TRANSCENDS CORPOREAL LIKENESS TO EXPRESS DEEPER TRUTHS ABOUT THE HUMAN CONDITION! THIS SCULPTURE IS ABOUT GRIEF AND SUFFERING!

ONE LOOK AT THE TORTURED COUNTENANCE OF THIS FIGURE CONFIRMS THAT THE ARTIST HAS DRUNK DEEPLY FROM THE CUP OF LIFE! THIS WORK SHALL ENDURE AND INSPIRE FUTURE GENERATIONS!

STILL MAKING SNOW ART?

YEP!

YESTERDAY YOUR SCULPTURE MELTED.

THIS TIME I'M TAKING *ADVANTAGE* OF MY MEDIUM'S IMPERMANENCE.

THIS SCULPTURE IS ABOUT TRANSIENCE. AS THIS FIGURE MELTS, IT INVITES THE VIEWER TO CONTEMPLATE THE EVANESCENCE OF LIFE. THIS PIECE SPEAKS TO THE HORROR OF OUR OWN MORTALITY!

HEY STUPID! IT'S TOO WARM TO BUILD A SNOWMAN! WHAT A DOPE! HA HA HA HA!

A PHILISTINE ON THE SIDEWALK.

GENIUS IS NEVER UNDERSTOOD IN ITS OWN TIME.

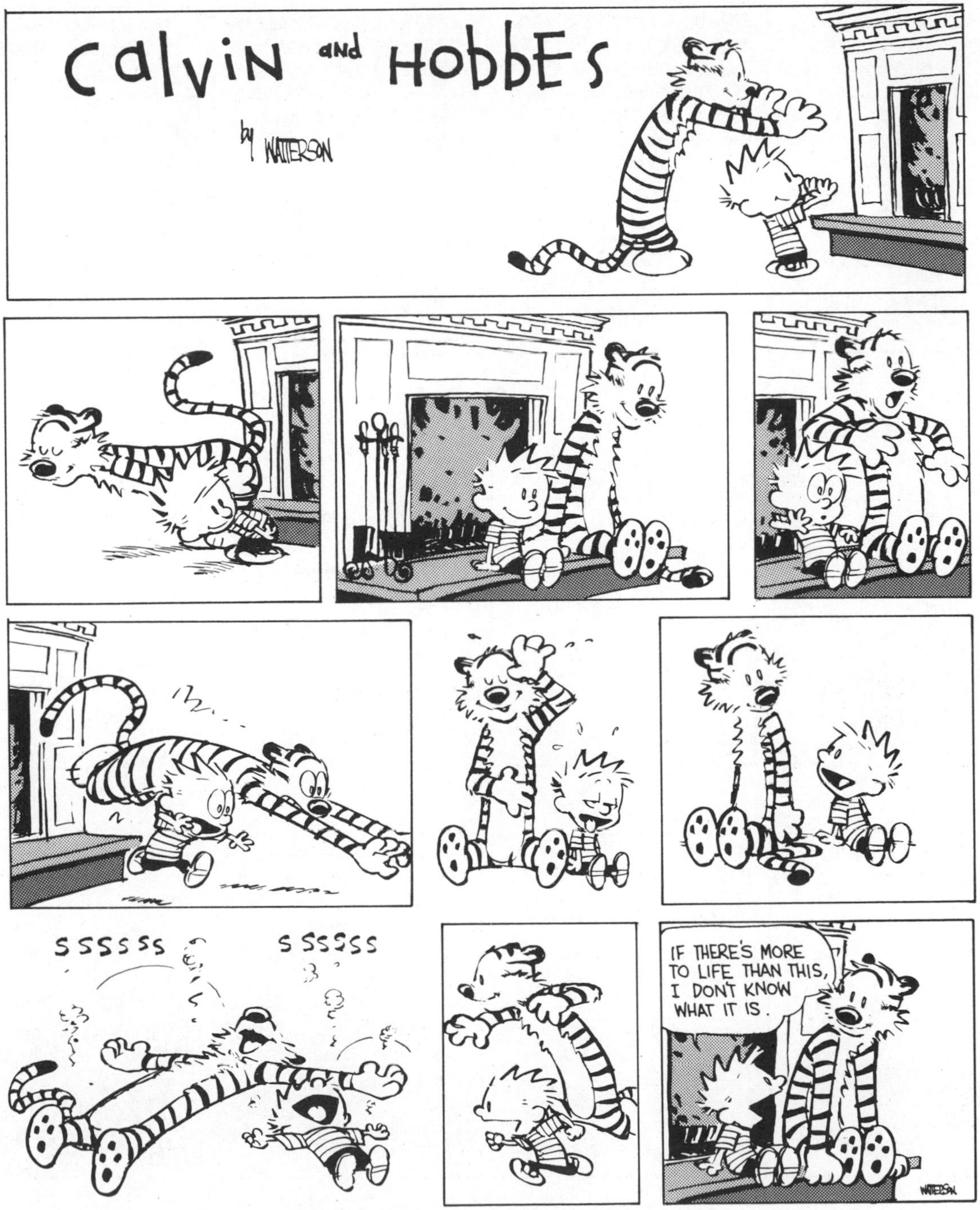
Calvin and HOBBES
by WATTERSON
SSSSSS
SSSSSS
IF THERE'S MORE TO LIFE THAN THIS, I DON'T KNOW WHAT IT IS.
WATTERSON

140 MILLION YEARS AGO, THE INCREDIBLE 'ULTRASAURS' WANDER THE EARTH! SOME WEIGH OVER 70 TONS, AND EVEN THE VICIOUS ALLOSAURS ARE NO MATCH FOR THESE GIANTS!

BUT WAIT! A DISTANT RUMBLING SENDS THE ULTRASAURS INTO A PANICKED STAMPEDE! IS IT A VOLCANO? IS IT AN EARTHQUAKE?

NO! IT'S...IT'S A CALVINOSAURUS!

NAMED AFTER THE RENOWNED PALEONTOLOGIST WHO DISCOVERED IT, THE HUGE CALVINOSAUR CAN EAT AN ULTRASAUR IN A SINGLE BITE!

PHOOEY! I NEVER FIND ANYTHING.

IT LOOKS LIKE YOU'VE HIT THE SEWER PIPE.

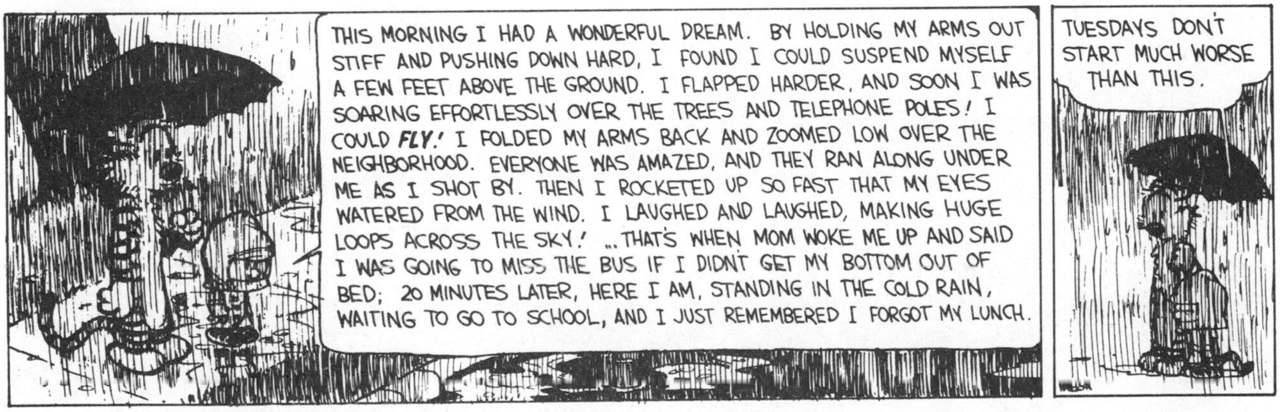

CALVIN and HOBBES

by WATTERSON

BEWARE! FALLING BUCKEYES

HERE COMES SOMEBODY!

THIS MEETING OF THE TOP SECRET CLUB G.R.O.S.S. (GET RID OF SLIMY GIRLS) WILL COME TO ORDER. TODAY THIS AUGUST ASSEMBLY WILL DECIDE WHETHER TO DEMOTE PRESIDENT HOBBES ON CHARGES OF HERESY!

HERESY?!

LET THE RECORD SHOW THAT THE DEFENDANT MADE AN *UN*DISPARAGING COMMENT ABOUT THE POSSIBLE MEMBERSHIP OF SUSIE DERKINS, AN ADMITTED GIRL AND ENEMY OF THIS CLUB.

LET THE RECORD *ALSO* SHOW THAT SUPREME DICTATOR-FOR-LIFE CALVIN IS A NINCOMPOOP.

OK, JUST FOR *THAT*, YOU'RE ALSO CHARGED WITH INSUBORDINATION! THIS COURT FINDS YOU GUILTY ON BOTH COUNTS AND STRIPS YOU OF YOUR TITLE!

HA! AS COURT STENOGRAPHER, I REFUSE TO ENTER THE VERDICT! IN FACT, I'M PRO-MOTING MYSELF TO "EL TIGRE NUMERO UNO"!

OH YEAH?! WELL THEN, I PROMOTE *MY*SELF TO "MOST HIGHEST, GRANDEST, EXALTED, UM, SUPREME, UH..

THERE! I WROTE "HOBBES EQUALS GREAT" IN THE OFFICIAL CLUB NOTEBOOK! NOW IT'S A LAW!

IT IS NOT! GIMME THAT!

HOPS = GRAT

HA HA HA! I'M WRITING "HOBBES EQUALS UGLY FUR BALL"! WHAT DO YOU THINK OF *THAT*?

OH HO! I TAKE THE SUPREME DICTATOR HAT! NOW *I'M* THE SUPREME DICTATOR!

YOU GIVE THAT BACK!

I DECLARE YOU NULL AND VOID!

TRUCE?

TRUCE.

WHAT A GREAT CLUB. TOO BAD WE DON'T HAVE MORE MEMBERS.

MAYBE WE SHOULD ALLOW SUSIE TO JOIN.

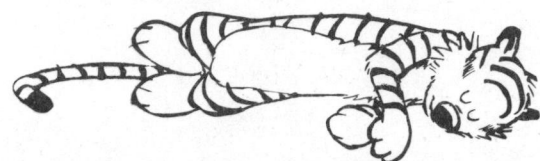

CALVIN and HOBBES

by WATTERSON

NYUP
NYUP

BOY, ROUGH LIFE, HUH? WHAT HAVE *YOU* DONE TODAY?!

PEOPLE!

WHERE DO WE KEEP THE EXTENSION CORDS?

IN THE PANTRY, ON THE BOTTOM SHELF.

WHERE DO WE KEEP THE BLADES FOR DAD'S ELECTRIC SAW?

IN THE... WHY DO YOU WANT TO KNOW?

HUH? OH, I'M JUST MAKING AN INVENTORY LIST SO WE'LL ALWAYS KNOW WHERE TO FIND THINGS.

I GET THE FEELING THERE WAS NO RIGHT ANSWER TO THAT QUESTION.

CALVIN, COME OUT FROM WHEREVER YOU'RE HIDING AND TAKE YOUR BATH!

DO YOU HEAR ME, CALVIN?! I MEAN NOW!

OH NO! LOOK AT YOU! AUGH! GET OFF THE RUG!

LIKE IT'S MY FAULT SHE HASN'T GOTTEN THE CHIMNEY SWEPT.

MOM! MOM! I JUST SAW THE FIRST ROBIN OF SPRING! CALL THE NEWSPAPER QUICK!

HA HA! A FRONT PAGE WRITE-UP! A COMMEMORATIVE PLAQUE! A CIVIC CEREMONY! ALL FOR ME! HOORAY! HOORAY!

OH BOY! SHOULD I PUT THE PRIZE MONEY IN A TRUST FUND, OR BLOW IT ALL AT ONCE? HA HA! I CAN'T BELIEVE I DID IT!

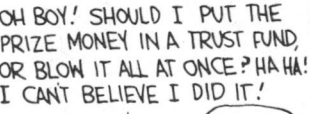

CALVIN...

IT'S A HARD, BITTER, CRUEL WORLD TO HAVE TO GROW UP IN, HOBBES.

CHEER UP! DID I TELL YOU I SAW A ROBIN YESTERDAY?

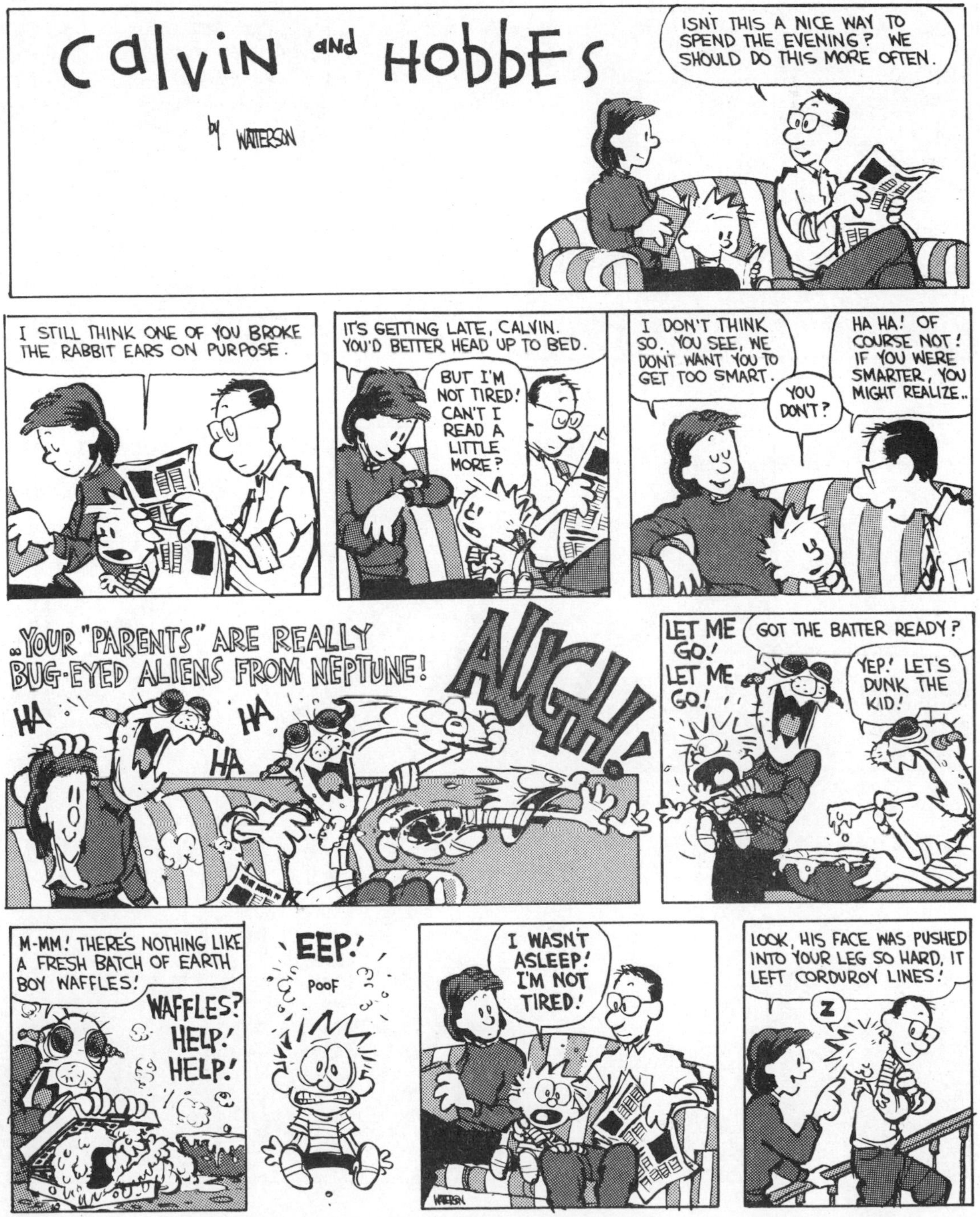
Calvin and HobbEs
by WATTERSON
ISN'T THIS A NICE WAY TO SPEND THE EVENING? WE SHOULD DO THIS MORE OFTEN.
I STILL THINK ONE OF YOU BROKE THE RABBIT EARS ON PURPOSE.
IT'S GETTING LATE, CALVIN. YOU'D BETTER HEAD UP TO BED.
BUT I'M NOT TIRED! CAN'T I READ A LITTLE MORE?
I DON'T THINK SO.. YOU SEE, WE DON'T WANT YOU TO GET TOO SMART.
YOU DON'T?
HA HA! OF COURSE NOT! IF YOU WERE SMARTER, YOU MIGHT REALIZE..
..YOUR "PARENTS" ARE REALLY BUG-EYED ALIENS FROM NEPTUNE!
HA
HA
HA
AUGH!
LET ME GO! LET ME GO!
GOT THE BATTER READY?
YEP! LET'S DUNK THE KID!
M-MM! THERE'S NOTHING LIKE A FRESH BATCH OF EARTH BOY WAFFLES!
WAFFLES? HELP! HELP!
EEP!
POOF
I WASN'T ASLEEP! I'M NOT TIRED!
WATTERSON
LOOK, HIS FACE WAS PUSHED INTO YOUR LEG SO HARD, IT LEFT CORDUROY LINES!
Z

WHAT ARE WE GOING TO *DO*, HOBBES? ROSALYN WILL BE HERE IN JUST A FEW HOURS!

DO YOU THINK SHE'LL REMEMBER HOW YOU LOCKED HER OUTSIDE LAST TIME?

IF SHE DOES, WE'RE DEAD! SHE'LL PROBABLY STICK MY HEAD ON A STAKE IN THE FRONT YARD AS A WARNING TO *OTHER* KIDS SHE BABY-SITS!

I'M ALMOST SURE THAT WOULD VIOLATE SOME ZONING ORDINANCE.

WELL NO MATTER WHAT, WE'RE IN BIG TROUBLE UNLESS WE THINK OF SOMETHING *FAST!*

I SUPPOSE WE COULD TRY BEING *GOOD.*

I MUST'VE GOTTEN WATER IN MY EAR. *WHAT* DID YOU SAY?

NOTHING. FORGET IT.

HI ROSALYN, COME ON IN. THANKS FOR COMING AGAIN.

NO TROUBLE.

HI ROSALYN! YOU DON'T NEED TO WORRY *THIS* TIME. CALVIN WILL BE ON HIS BEST BEHAVIOR TONIGHT.

EVEN SO, I'D LIKE AN ADVANCE.

AN ADVANCE? BUT... BUT...

DEAR, MAY I SPEAK WITH YOU A MOMENT?

BUT WE *GAVE* HER AN ADVANCE ON TONIGHT WHEN SHE *LEFT* LAST TIME!

I DON'T CARE. JUST PAY WHAT IT TAKES TO GET US OUT OF HERE!

OK, WE'RE GOING. ...AND CALVIN?

YES?

GCKKHHK!

I THINK I'LL SIT IN THE MIDDLE OF THE FLOOR AND LOOK AT THE WALL TONIGHT.

GOOD. I'LL TELL YOU WHEN IT'S BEDTIME.

THERE GOES ROSALYN AROUND THE HOUSE AGAIN. SHE STILL DOESN'T KNOW YOU SNEAKED BACK INSIDE.

NOW I'LL CHANGE BACK INTO MY SECRET IDENTITY ALTER EGO!

UH OH. SHE SAW THE LIGHT ON IN THIS ROOM. SHE'S COMING IN!

QUICK! GET IN THE COVERS! PRETEND WE'VE JUST BEEN READING IN BED!

BUT SHE KNOWS YOU ATTACKED HER AND RAN OUTSIDE HALF AN HOUR AGO!

THAT WAS *STUPENDOUS MAN*, NOT MILD-MANNERED CALVIN! *I'VE* BEEN IN BED WITH MY PJs ON SINCE 8:00.

YOU THINK SHE'S GOING TO BELIEVE *THAT?*

MY COVERS ARE HERE. MY PAJAMAS ARE *HERE.* IT'S AS PLAIN AS CAN BE!

ALL RIGHT! *I* FOUND YOU!

FOUND?? WHY, WHAT DO YOU MEAN? I'VE BEEN IN BED READING ALL EVENING WITH HOBBES.

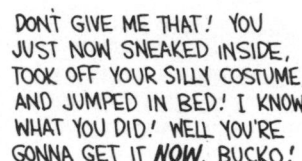

DON'T GIVE ME THAT! YOU JUST NOW SNEAKED INSIDE, TOOK OFF YOUR SILLY COSTUME, AND JUMPED IN BED! I KNOW WHAT YOU DID! WELL YOU'RE GONNA GET IT *NOW*, BUCKO!

OH YEAH? WHAT ARE YOU GOING TO DO TO ME, HUH? YOU CAN'T SEND ME TO BED WHEN I'M ALREADY *IN* BED! SORRY TO SPOIL YOUR FUN, YOU EEL!

OK, DOWNSTAIRS! *MARCH!*

HEY, YOU CAN'T TAKE ME *OUT* OF BED! I NEED MY *SLEEP!* HEY! HEY!

WHILE YOUR DAD IS TAKING ROSALYN HOME, PERHAPS *YOU'D* LIKE TO EXPLAIN WHAT HAPPENED TONIGHT.

GOSH MOM, WHAT'S TO TELL? AT 8:00, I PUT ON MY PAJAMAS, BRUSHED MY TEETH AND WENT STRAIGHT TO BED. NOTHING HAPPENED.

AND THIS?

UH... *LIES!* ALL LIES! ROSALYN MADE ME DO THAT JUST SO I'D GET IN TROUBLE! SHE HATES KIDS! NONE OF THAT IS TRUE! I WENT STRAIGHT TO BED!

NICE TRY, PINOCCHIO.

WELL WHO WOULD'VE THOUGHT ROSALYN WOULD MAKE ME WRITE A FULL CONFESSION?!

CALVIN and HOBBES by WATTERSON

HMPH!

LIFE'S DISAPPOINTMENTS ARE HARDER TO TAKE WHEN YOU DON'T KNOW ANY SWEAR WORDS.

BOY, I'M IN A ROTTEN MOOD. THE WORLD HAD JUST BETTER LOOK OUT!

HEY YOU, YOU'RE IN MY WAY! MOVE IT!

WHAT'S THE MATTER? DID YOU GO DEAF?! GET OUT OF MY WAY! SCRAM!

C'MON, HURRY UP! YOU THINK I'VE GOT ALL DAY?!

NOW ARE YOU GOING TO STEP ASIDE, OR *WHAT*?! I'M COMING THROUGH!

MMPH! GGGHH! WHAT ARE YOU DOING?! I *SAID* MOVE ASIDE!!

DOGGONE IT, WHEN I SAY *MOVE*, I EXPECT YOU TO JUMP! *MOVE!*

MOVE! MOVE! MOVE! MOVE! MOVE!

HEY! PUT ME DOWN! WHERE ARE YOU TAKING ME?! I DEMAND AN EXPLANA... HEY, IS THAT A MUD HOLE?! YOU'D BETTER NOT! YOU HEAR ME?!

SEE WHY I'M IN SUCH A BAD MOOD??

93

NO TV FOR A WEEK! WHAT INJUSTICE!

THEY THINK THEY'VE WON, BUT THEY HAVEN'T!

I'LL SHOW 'EM! I *REFUSE* TO LEARN A LESSON!

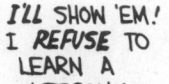

I'M INDOMITABLE! THEY CAN'T CHANGE ME!

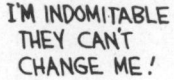

I'LL SIT IN FRONT OF THE TV ALL WEEK, EVEN IF I CAN'T TURN IT ON!

DAD, WILL YOU EXPLAIN THE THEORY OF RELATIVITY TO ME? I DON'T UNDERSTAND WHY TIME GOES SLOWER AT GREAT SPEED.

IT'S BECAUSE YOU KEEP CHANGING TIME ZONES. SEE, IF YOU FLY TO CALIFORNIA, YOU GAIN THREE HOURS ON A FIVE-HOUR FLIGHT, RIGHT?

SO IF YOU GO AT THE SPEED OF LIGHT, YOU GAIN *MORE* TIME, BECAUSE IT DOESN'T TAKE AS LONG TO GET THERE. OF COURSE, THE THEORY OF RELATIVITY ONLY WORKS IF YOU'RE GOING WEST.

GEE, THAT'S NOT WHAT MOM SAID AT **ALL**! SHE MUST BE TOTALLY OFF HER ROCKER.

WELL, WE MEN ARE BETTER AT ABSTRACT REASONING. GO TELL HER THAT.

MOM, CAN WE GO OUT TO THE HIGHWAY?

DO WHAT?

SEE, I'LL PUT ON MY ROLLER SKATES AND TIE A ROPE FROM THE CAR BUMPER TO MY WAIST. THEN WHEN I GIVE YOU THE HIGH FIVE, YOU PATCH OUT WHILE I RIDE BEHIND AT 55 MPH!

WHAT DO YOU SAY? CAN WE GO?

I SURE WISH *YOU* COULD DRIVE.

ACE PILOT SPACEMAN SPIFF CRUISES LOW OVER THE PLANET AT HIGH SPEED!

I WONDER WHAT THIS "E" ON THE FUEL GAUGE MEANS.

THE INTREPID SPACEMAN SPIFF LANDS ON PLANET GORZARG-5!

OUR HERO SETS OFF ACROSS THE DESOLATE TERRAIN IN SEARCH OF HELP! IN THE DISTANCE, METHANE CLOUDS RAIN SODIUM HYDROXIDE, A CAUSTIC ALKALI!

OH NO! THE DOWNPOUR WAS TOO HEAVY FOR THE GROUND TO ABSORB! A STEAMING RIVER OF CORROSIVE LIQUID RUSHES TOWARD OUR HERO!

THE BRAVE SPACEMAN SPIFF SCRAMBLES TO HIGHER GROUND, BUT THE FLOOD CONTINUES TO RISE!

OUR HERO IS TRAPPED! IT'S ONLY A MATTER OF TIME UNTIL THE FOAMING, NOXIOUS WASH CLEANS THE MEAT FROM SPIFF'S BONES! HOW COULD — THINGS EVER GET WORSE?!

AUGHH! AN ALIEN COMES TO PUSH HIM IN!

FOR HEAVEN'S SAKE, CALVIN! JUST GET IN!

Panel 1: Hey, lookit the sissy who didn't sign up for recess baseball! / I'M NOT A SISSY!

Panel 2: Oh yeah? You'd rather play dolls on the playground with girls. / I WASN'T PLAYING WITH DOLLS!

Panel 3: Sure you weren't! Let me see your Barbie doll, you sissy wimp! / I'M NOT A WIMP! IN FACT, I WAS GOING TO THE OFFICE TO SIGN UP FOR BASEBALL RIGHT NOW!

Panel 4: THEN AGAIN, IF I'M NOT A WIMP, WHY AM I TAKING THE PATH OF LEAST RESISTANCE? / OFFICE

Panel 5: I SIGNED UP TO PLAY BASEBALL EVERY RECESS, AND I DON'T EVEN *LIKE* BASEBALL THAT MUCH.

Panel 6: I MEAN, IT'S FUN PLAYING BASEBALL WITH JUST *YOU*, BECAUSE WE BOTH GET TO PITCH, BAT, RUN AND CATCH ALL AT ONCE. WE GET TO *DO* EVERYTHING.

Panel 7: MOSTLY WE JUST ARGUE OVER THE RULES WE MAKE UP! THAT'S THE PART *I* LIKE! / BUT THIS WILL BE WITH *TEAMS* AND ASSIGNED POSITIONS AND AN UMPIRE! IT'S *BORING* PLAYING IT THE *REAL* WAY!

Panel 8: DO YOU EVEN KNOW *HOW* TO PLAY THE REAL WAY? / SEE, THAT'S *ANOTHER* PROBLEM! SUPPOSE THEY MAKE ME A HALFBACK. CAN I TACKLE THE SHORTSTOP OR NOT?

Panel 9: I HEAR YOU SIGNED UP TO PLAY SOFTBALL AT RECESS. / YEAH, BUT I DIDN'T EVEN WANT TO. I JUST DID IT TO STOP GETTING TEASED.

Panel 10: WELL, SPORTS ARE GOOD FOR YOU. THEY TEACH TEAMWORK AND COOPERATION. YOU LEARN HOW TO WIN GRACIOUSLY AND ACCEPT DEFEAT. IT BUILDS CHARACTER.

Panel 11: EVERY TIME I'VE BUILT CHARACTER, I'VE REGRETTED IT! I DON'T *WANT* TO LEARN TEAMWORK! I DON'T *WANT* TO LEARN ABOUT WINNING AND LOSING! HECK, I DON'T EVEN WANT TO *COMPETE*! WHAT'S WRONG WITH JUST HAVING FUN BY YOURSELF, HUH?!

Panel 12: WHEN YOU GROW UP, IT'S NOT ALLOWED. / ALL THE MORE REASON I SHOULD DO IT *NOW*!

I SEE YOU'RE BRINGING A GLOVE TODAY. DID YOU SIGN UP FOR RECESS BASEBALL?

YEAH, DON'T REMIND ME.

YOU'RE LUCKY THAT GIRLS DON'T HAVE TO PUT UP WITH THIS NONSENSE. IF A GIRL DOESN'T WANT TO PLAY SPORTS, THAT'S FINE!

BUT IF A GUY DOESN'T SPEND HIS AFTERNOONS CHASING SOME STUPID BALL, HE'S CALLED A WIMP! YOU GIRLS HAVE IT EASY!

ON THE OTHER HAND, BOYS AREN'T EXPECTED TO SPEND THEIR LIVES 20 POUNDS UNDERWEIGHT.

AND IF YOU DON'T PLAY SPORTS, YOU DON'T GET TO MAKE BEER COMMERCIALS!

MR. LOCKJAW? I'M CALVIN. I'M SUPPOSED TO BE ON TEAM FIVE NOW.

OH YES, YOU'RE THE ONE WHO SIGNED UP LATE. HMM... OK, YOU GO PLAY LEFT FIELD.

LEFT FIELD. OK, I KNOW THAT. LET'S SEE, IF I'M HERE, THEN LEFT FIELD WOULD BE...

THAT WAY. PLAY DEEP LEFT FIELD.

I GUESS THIS IS PRETTY DEEP.

I THINK BASEBALL IS THE MOST BORING GAME IN THE WORLD. I'VE BEEN STANDING OUT HERE IN DEEP LEFT FIELD ALL THIS TIME, AND NOT A SINGLE BALL HAS COME OUT HERE!

ACTUALLY, I SUPPOSE THAT'S JUST AS WELL. I DON'T KNOW WHAT BASE TO THROW TO ANYWAY. IN FACT, I'M NOT EVEN SURE I CAN THROW THAT FAR.

HEY, WHAT'S EVERYONE DOING? ARE PEOPLE SWITCHING TEAMS, OR WHAT? THE GUYS AT BAT ARE NOW OUT HERE!

WELL, I'M SURE SOMEONE WOULD TELL ME IF I WAS SUPPOSED TO BE DOING ANYTHING DIFFERENT.

OUR HERO, THE FEARLESS SPACEMAN SPIFF, IS MAROONED ON THE MOST DISTANT PLANET IN THE GALAXY!

THERE'S NO HOPE OF RESCUE FROM THIS BLEAK AND ISOLATED WORLD!

OH, WHAT A DESOLATE PLACE TO BE TRAPPED! SPIFF TRIES DESPERATELY TO REPAIR HIS DISABLED SPACECRAFT!

CRACK

HIGH FLY TO LEFT FIELD! WHO'S OUT THERE?!

OUR HERO PAUSES. THERE'S SOME COMMOTION ON THE HORIZON. *ALIENS!* SPIFF GRABS HIS BLASTER!

WHERE'S THE LEFT FIELDER?!

SOMEBODY CATCH IT!

LEFT FIELD?! HEY, THAT'S *ME!*

WOW! A HIGH FLY RIGHT TO ME! I GOT IT! I GOT IT!

I CAUGHT IT!!

HE CAUGHT IT! IT'S AN OUT!

WAP!

I'M JUST A NATURAL ATHLETE, I GUESS.

HEY, WHO'S *HE?*

ISN'T HE ON THE OTHER TEAM?

HEY, LOOK WHO MADE THE OUT!

IT'S *CALVIN!*

HECK, IT WAS NOTHING, GUYS. WHEN YOU'RE IN TOP PHYSICAL CONDITION LIKE ME, YOU CAN...

YOU MORON! WHAT WERE YOU DOING IN THE OUTFIELD?! IT'S A NEW INNING! WE'RE UP TO *BAT!*

HUH?

YOU CAUGHT THE BALL FOR THE WRONG TEAM! YOU GOT OUR OWN GUY OUT! WHAT A DWEEB! WHAT A JERK! WHAT AN *IDIOT!*

OOPS, I DROPPED THE CATCH. IT DOESN'T COUNT NOW, RIGHT?

GET HIM OFF OUR TEAM, MR. LOCKJAW!

CAN I HIT HIM WITH THE BAT? PLEASE? PLEASE??

100

TODAY FOR "SHOW AND TELL", I HAVE A SOUVENIR FROM THE AFTERLIFE! YES, YOU HEARD RIGHT! EQUALLY AMAZING IS MY OWN STORY OF YESTERDAY AFTERNOON, WHEN I ACTUALLY DIED OF BOREDOM!

I WAS DOING MY HOMEWORK, WHEN SUDDENLY I COLLAPSED! I FELT MYSELF RISING, AND I COULD SEE MY CRUMPLED BODY ON THE FLOOR. I DRIFTED UP IN A SHAFT OF LIGHT AND I ENTERED THE NEXT WORLD!

EVENTUALLY, MY HEART STARTED AGAIN AND I CAME BACK TO LIFE ... BUT NOT BEFORE BRINGING *THIS* BACK!

A YO-YO?

IT WAS PRETTY BORING *THERE*, TOO.

LET'S HAVE A LOOK AT THAT HOMEWORK.

AND SO, HAVING EATEN HER FILL, THE MOTHER BIRD RETURNS TO HER NEST...

.. WHERE SHE REGURGITATES THE WORMS TO FEED HER HUNGRY BROOD.

...SIGHHHHH...

CALVIN, PAY ATTENTION!

NUGH

THERE'S NO HEAD REST ON THIS CHAIR! I SHOULD SUE FOR WHIPLASH!

Calvin and Hobbes

by WATTERSON

ARE YOU GOING TO READ CALVIN A STORY?

ONLY IF IT'S NOT THAT AWFUL "HAMSTER HUEY AND THE GOOEY KABLOOIE".

OH, BUT YOU LOOK SO *CUTE* DOING THE "HAPPY HAMSTER HOP"!

I DON'T *WANT* TO LOOK CUTE!!

WHAT STORY WOULD YOU LIKE TONIGHT, CALVIN?

I WANT A STORY ABOUT HOBBES AND ME.

OK...HMM... LET'S SEE... ONCE THERE WAS A BOY NAMED CALVIN WHO LIVED WITH A TIGER NAMED HOBBES.

THIS IS GREAT!

TODAY THEY GOT UP AT THE CRACK OF DAWN AND MADE A HUGE RUCKUS RUNNING **UP** THE STAIRS, GALUMP, GALUMP, GALUMP, AND SLIDING **DOWN** AGAIN, BUMP, BUMP BUMP, BUMP.'

YEAH, THEN THE **BIG BAD DAD** YELLED THAT IF WE DIDN'T KNOCK IT OFF, HE'D MAIL US TO **PLUTO** THIRD CLASS!

WHO'S TELLING THIS STORY, YOU OR ME?

YOU *DID* SAY THAT! DON'T TRY TO DENY IT!

SO FINALLY, CALVIN GOT THE HINT AND HE WENT TO ROT HIS INNARDS WITH CHOCOLATE CEREAL, AND TO ROT HIS BRAIN WATCHING CARTOONS.

HEY! *NO* EDITOR- IALS!

AT LAST CALVIN AND HOBBES WENT OUTSIDE, AND IT WAS NICE AND QUIET IN THE HOUSE AGAIN. AT LEAST FOR A WHILE. WELL, GOOD NIGHT.'

GOOD NIGHT?! THAT'S NOT THE END! YOU DIDN'T EVEN GET US TO LUNCHTIME!

THAT'S RIGHT... IT'S NOT THE END OF THE STORY. THIS STORY DOESN'T *HAVE* AN END. YOU AND HOBBES WILL WRITE MORE OF IT TOMORROW AND EVERY DAY AFTER. BUT NOW IT'S TIME TO SLEEP, SO GOOD NIGHT.

OH! OK, GOOD NIGHT.

THIS *IS* A GOOD STORY ABOUT US IF IT DOESN'T END.' THAT'S THE KIND OF STORY I LIKE BEST.' GOOD NIGHT, OL' BUDDY!

ME TOO! SEE YOU TOMORROW!

Calvin and Hobbes

by WATTERSON

I'M FREEEEEEEEEEEEEEEEEE

I'VE COME UP WITH A NEW SYSTEM FOR DOING HOMEWORK. I CALL IT "EFFECTIVE TIME MANAGEMENT," OR "ETM" FOR SHORT.

I'VE DRAWN UP A SCHEDULE FOR EACH SCHOOL SUBJECT, AND I USE THIS KITCHEN TIMER TO MONITOR MY PACE.

THANKS TO ETM, I'M MUCH MORE EFFICIENT, AND MY WORK GOES FASTER!

RINGG

THERE! MY MATH MINUTE IS UP! SET THE CLOCK FOR MY SPELLING ASSIGNMENT, OK?

UM, YOUR SCHEDULE CALLS FOR SMALLER TIME INCREMENTS THAN THIS CLOCK CAN MEASURE.

NO I WON'T TAKE A PICTURE OF YOU.

KA

ZAM!

WHAT?

CALVIN and HOBBES

by WATTERSON

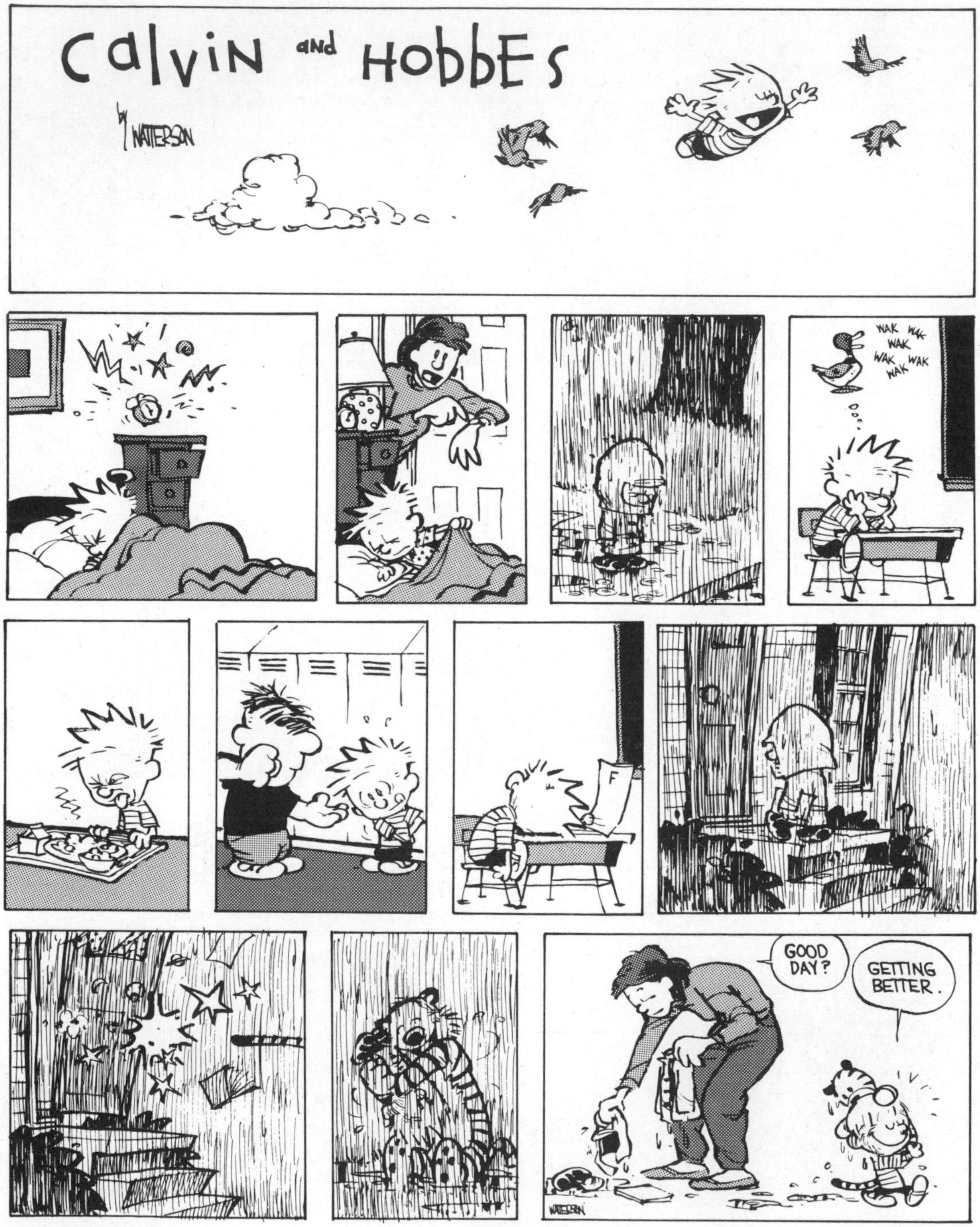
Calvin and HOBBES
by WATTERSON
WAK WAK WAK WAK WAK WAK
F
GOOD DAY?
GETTING BETTER.
WATTERSON

ON DISTANT PLANET ZARK, WE FIND THE EMPTY RED SPACECRAFT OF OUR HERO, THE BOLD *SPACEMAN SPIFF!*

UH OH! UP AHEAD, THE ROCKS ARE CHARRED WITH DEATH RAY BLASTS! A VIOLENT STRUGGLE TOOK PLACE HERE!

AND ONLY THE TRACKS OF A LARGE, SINISTER ALIEN LEAVE THE SCENE! WHAT HAS HAPPENED TO THE EARTHLING EXPLORER?

CALVIN, THIS IS HUMILIATING!!

I DON'T WANT TO GO! PUT ME DOWN!

SPACEMAN SPIFF IS BEING HELD PRISONER BY HIDEOUS ALIENS! WHAT DO THEY WANT WITH HIM?

SPIFF IS SOON TO FIND OUT! OUR HERO IS CALLED BEFORE THE ALIEN POTENTATE!

..WHERE IT BECOMES CLEAR THAT SPIFF IS ABOUT TO BE *SACRIFICED*...

..TO APPEASE THE EVIL GOD THEY CALL "NOLLIJ"!

UP TO THE BLACKBOARD. HURRY UP.

STARING DEATH IN THE FACE, OUR HERO THINKS FAST.

11 - 4 =

INCHING CLOSER TO THE SACRIFICIAL PIT, SPIFF SLOWLY AND SMOOTHLY REACHES FOR THE TINY ATOM BLASTER CONCEALED IN HIS BELT!

YAA! ALL RIGHT, YOU BLOODSUCKING, MUTANT CHROMOSOMAL DISASTERS! NOBODY MOVE! I'M OUTTA HERE!

CALVIN, GIVE ME THAT RUBBER BAND RIGHT THIS MINUTE!

I SAID NOBODY MOVE!

SPIFF ESCAPES! THE DANK AND SMELLY CORRIDORS OF THE ALIEN FORTRESS ARE DESERTED! ALL THE ALIENS HAD GATHERED FOR THE SPECTACLE OF OUR HERO'S DEMISE!

THE FEARLESS SPACE EXPLORER MAKES IT TO THE PLANET SURFACE, BUT THE ALIEN QUEEN IS IN PURSUIT!

CALVIN, GET BACK HERE!

SPIFF JUMPS INTO THE COCKPIT, PRESSURIZES THE LAUNCH THRUSTERS, AND...

BLASTS OFF! OUR HERO IS SAFE!

Tomorrow: OR *IS* HE ?!?

CALVIN! WHAT ARE YOU DOING HOME?! IT'S NOT EVEN NOON!

UH, THEY LET US OUT EARLY TODAY. THERE WAS, UM, A GAS LEAK.

WHAT?! DOES ANYONE KNOW YOU LEFT?! I'M CALLING THE SCHOOL.

DON'T WASTE YOUR TIME! EVERYONE WAS EVACUATED! THERE'S NOBODY THERE!

HELLO? ELEMENTARY SCHOOL OFFICE, PLEASE.

OUR HERO HADN'T COUNTED ON RUNNING INTO A ZARK ENFORCER SHIP! SPIFF'S EVASIVE MANEUVERS COME TO NAUGHT! THIS COULD BE THE END!

BOY, I SURE GOT IN BIG TROUBLE *TODAY!* MOM HIT THE ROOF WHEN SHE FOUND OUT I JUST LEFT SCHOOL.

WHAT HAPPENED?

SHE DROVE ME BACK AND WE HAD TO TALK TO MY TEACHER *AND* THE PRINCIPAL! THEY TALKED ABOUT MY STUDY HABITS, AND NOW I'VE GOT EXTRA HOMEWORK!

OOH.

AND DAD IS GOING TO CHECK IT EVERY NIGHT TO MAKE SURE IT'S DONE RIGHT! CAN YOU BELIEVE IT ?!

SO TRY TO DO AN EXTRA GOOD JOB NOW, OK?

YOU'RE LUCKY TIGERS ARE SO SMART.

CALVIN and HOBBES

by WATTERSON

OLLY-WOLLY POLLIWOGGY UMP-BUMP FIZZ!

HEY!

HA HA! I STOLE YOUR FLAG!

BUT I HIT YOU WITH THE CALVIN BALL! YOU HAVE TO PUT THE FLAG BACK AND SING THE "I'M VERY SORRY" SONG!

I DON'T HAVE TO SING THE SONG! I WAS IN THE "NO SONG" ZONE!

NO YOU WEREN'T. I TOUCHED THE "OPPOSITE POLE", SO THE "NO SONG ZONE" IS NOW A "SONG ZONE"!

I DIDN'T SEE YOU TOUCH THE OPPOSITE POLE! YOU HAVE TO DECLARE IT!

I DECLARED IT OPPOSITELY BY NOT DECLARING IT. START SINGING.

"HERE'S THE 'VERY SORRY SONGG'. WON'T YOU HELP AND SING ALONGG?"

BUM BUM BUM

I BLEW IT! ..... I KNEW IT! ..... I'M VERY VERY SORRY THAT I TOOK YOUR PRECIOUS FLAAGGG!

HE'S SORRY! SO SORRY! JUST DON'T DO IT ANY MORE, YOU SCURVY SCALAWAAGGG!

I'M FREE! I GET FREE PASSAGE TO WICKET FIVE!

NO, THAT'S WHAT WE DID LAST TIME, REMEMBER?

OH YEAH. HMM.

OK, THE NEW RULE IS WE HAVE TO JUMP EVERYWHERE UNTIL SOMEONE FINDS THE BONUS BOX!

THAT'S GOOD!

THE ONLY PERMANENT RULE IN CALVINBALL IS THAT YOU CAN'T PLAY IT THE SAME WAY TWICE!

THE SCORE IS STILL Q TO 12!

ANOTHER PLANET, ANOTHER SWEEPING PANORAMA OF INDESCRIBABLE GRANDEUR!

THE INCREDIBLE SPACEMAN SPIFF ZOOMS TO THE SURFACE OF AHNOOIE-4!

TOUCHING DOWN, OUR HERO SETS OFF TO SEARCH FOR SENTIENT LIFE!

ALAS, SPACEMAN SPIFF ONLY DISCOVERS A HIDEOUS BLOB SO MONUMENTALLY STUPID THAT IT JUST STARES STRAIGHT AHEAD, COMPLETELY UNAWARE OF ANYTHING AROUND IT!

COMPASSIONATELY, OUR HERO DECIDES TO PUT THE BLOB OUT OF ITS MISERY. SPIFF SETS HIS BLASTER ON "LIQUEFY."

EWW! MISS WORMWOOD! CALVIN'S SHOOTING SPIT BALLS!

PERPLEXED BY THE BLOB'S RESILIENCE, SPIFF ADDS MORE JUICE AND PREPARES TO FIRE AGAIN!

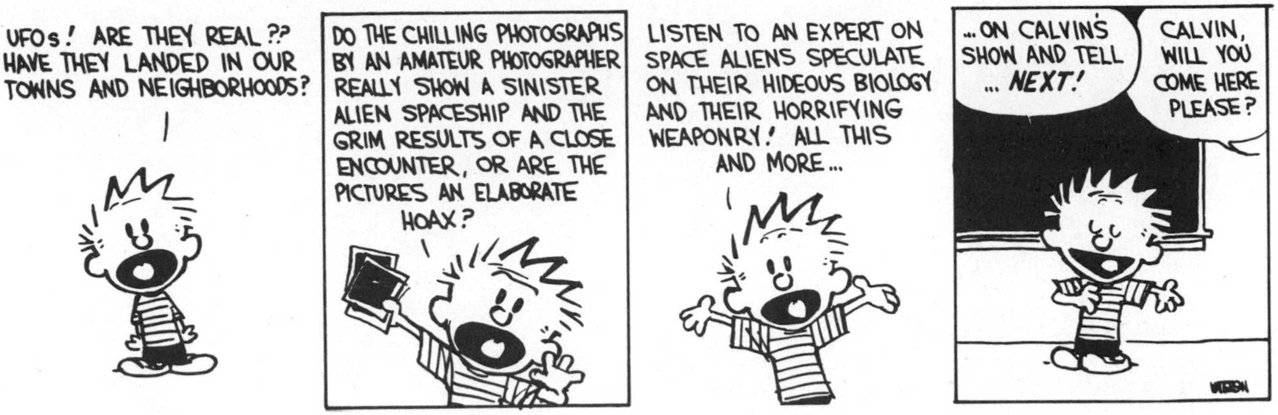
UFOs! ARE THEY REAL?? HAVE THEY LANDED IN OUR TOWNS AND NEIGHBORHOODS?
DO THE CHILLING PHOTOGRAPHS BY AN AMATEUR PHOTOGRAPHER REALLY SHOW A SINISTER ALIEN SPACESHIP AND THE GRIM RESULTS OF A CLOSE ENCOUNTER, OR ARE THE PICTURES AN ELABORATE HOAX?
LISTEN TO AN EXPERT ON SPACE ALIENS SPECULATE ON THEIR HIDEOUS BIOLOGY AND THEIR HORRIFYING WEAPONRY! ALL THIS AND MORE...
...ON CALVIN'S SHOW AND TELL ... NEXT!
CALVIN, WILL YOU COME HERE PLEASE?

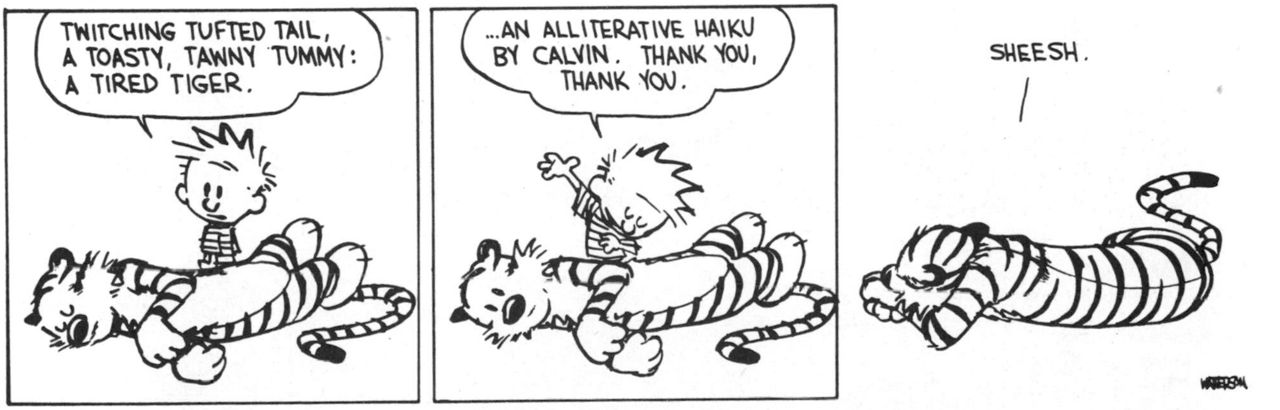
TWITCHING TUFTED TAIL, A TOASTY, TAWNY TUMMY: A TIRED TIGER.
...AN ALLITERATIVE HAIKU BY CALVIN. THANK YOU, THANK YOU.
SHEESH.

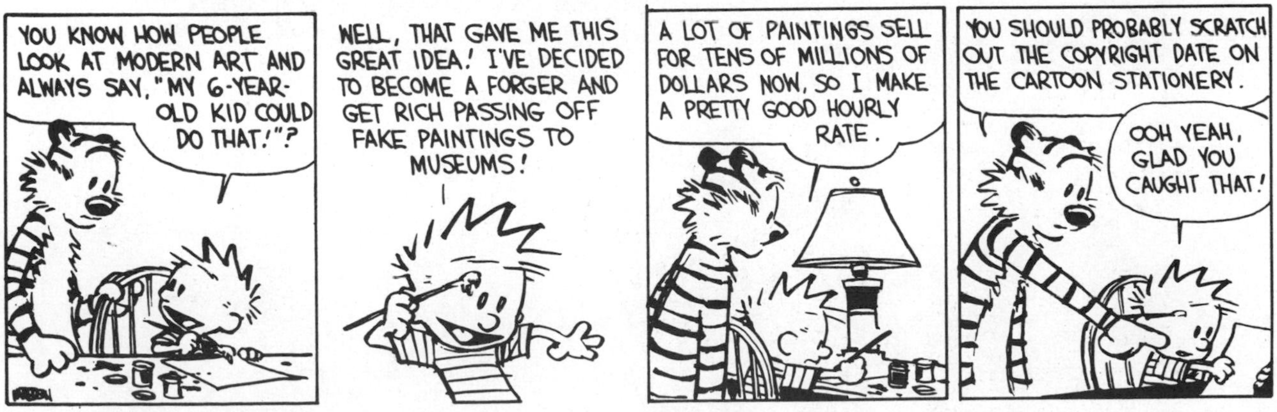
YOU KNOW HOW PEOPLE LOOK AT MODERN ART AND ALWAYS SAY, "MY 6-YEAR-OLD KID COULD DO THAT!"?
WELL, THAT GAVE ME THIS GREAT IDEA! I'VE DECIDED TO BECOME A FORGER AND GET RICH PASSING OFF FAKE PAINTINGS TO MUSEUMS!
A LOT OF PAINTINGS SELL FOR TENS OF MILLIONS OF DOLLARS NOW, SO I MAKE A PRETTY GOOD HOURLY RATE.
YOU SHOULD PROBABLY SCRATCH OUT THE COPYRIGHT DATE ON THE CARTOON STATIONERY.
OOH YEAH, GLAD YOU CAUGHT THAT!

Calvin and Hobbes

by Watterson

HISTORICAL MARKER "CALVIN'S HOUSE" IN JANUARY, SOME 40 SNOWMEN MET A GRUESOME FATE ON THIS SPOT.

EVERY DAY I LOOK FOR A MOVING VAN HERE.

KNOCK KNOCK

GREAT MOONS OF NEPTUNE! A FOOL MORTAL FEMALE!

CALVIN?

I'M NOT CALVIN! I'M STUPENDOUS MAN! FRIEND OF FREEDOM! OPPONENT OF OPPRESSION!

UH HUH. WHAT ARE YOU DOING?

I WAS JUST ABOUT TO USE MY STUPENDOUS POWERS TO LIBERATE SOME COOKIES BEING HELD HOSTAGE ON THE TOP SHELF OF THE PANTRY! NOW IF YOU'LL EXCUSE ME, DUTY CALLS!

SLAM!

A BOLT OF CRIMSON STREAKS ACROSS THE SKY! THE MAN OF MEGA-MIGHT IS OFF TO SAVE THE DAY!

DID THEY HAVE AN EGG YOU COULD BORROW?

NO ONE WAS HOME, MOM.

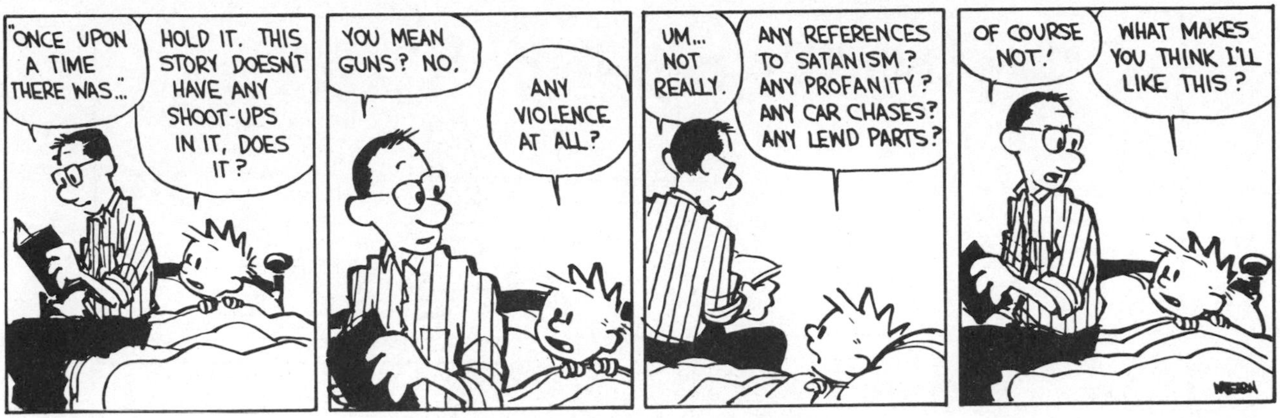
"ONCE UPON A TIME THERE WAS..."
HOLD IT. THIS STORY DOESN'T HAVE ANY SHOOT-UPS IN IT, DOES IT?
YOU MEAN GUNS? NO.
ANY VIOLENCE AT ALL?
UM... NOT REALLY.
ANY REFERENCES TO SATANISM? ANY PROFANITY? ANY CAR CHASES? ANY LEWD PARTS?
OF COURSE NOT!
WHAT MAKES YOU THINK I'LL LIKE THIS?

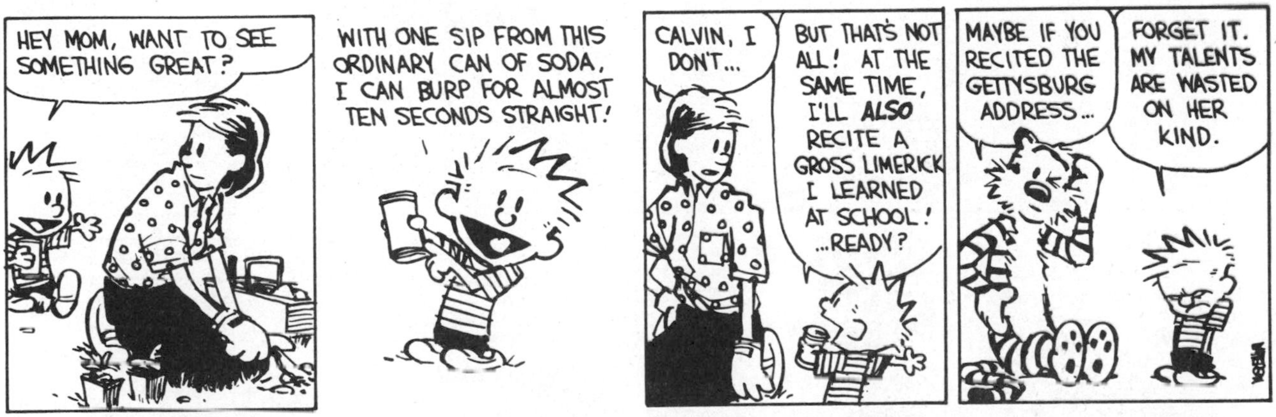
HEY MOM, WANT TO SEE SOMETHING GREAT?
WITH ONE SIP FROM THIS ORDINARY CAN OF SODA, I CAN BURP FOR ALMOST TEN SECONDS STRAIGHT!
CALVIN, I DON'T...
BUT THAT'S NOT ALL! AT THE SAME TIME, I'LL ALSO RECITE A GROSS LIMERICK I LEARNED AT SCHOOL! ...READY?
MAYBE IF YOU RECITED THE GETTYSBURG ADDRESS...
FORGET IT. MY TALENTS ARE WASTED ON HER KIND.

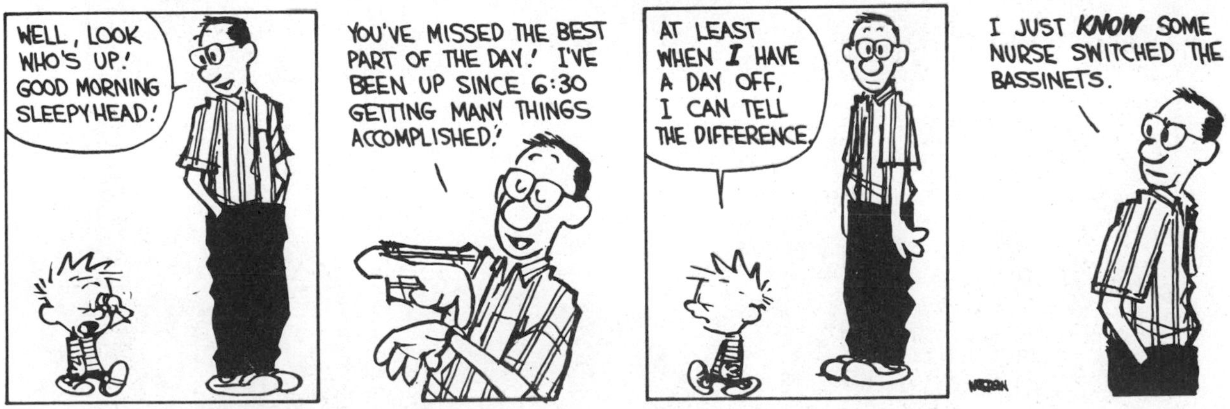
WELL, LOOK WHO'S UP! GOOD MORNING SLEEPYHEAD!
YOU'VE MISSED THE BEST PART OF THE DAY! I'VE BEEN UP SINCE 6:30 GETTING MANY THINGS ACCOMPLISHED!
AT LEAST WHEN I HAVE A DAY OFF, I CAN TELL THE DIFFERENCE.
I JUST KNOW SOME NURSE SWITCHED THE BASSINETS.

CLICK.

PANDER TO ME!

PLAYING A RECORD? I'LL SHOW YOU SOMETHING INTERESTING.

COMPARE A POINT ON THE LABEL WITH A POINT ON THE RECORD'S OUTER EDGE. THEY BOTH MAKE A COMPLETE CIRCLE IN THE SAME AMOUNT OF TIME, RIGHT?

YEAH...

BUT THE POINT ON THE RECORD'S EDGE HAS TO MAKE A BIGGER CIRCLE IN THE SAME TIME, SO IT GOES FASTER. SEE, TWO POINTS ON ONE DISK MOVE AT TWO SPEEDS, EVEN THOUGH THEY BOTH MAKE THE SAME REVOLUTIONS PER MINUTE!

ON YOUR MARK... GET SET... GO!

I'M GOING SO SLOW, I'M MOVING BACKWARD! I'M WINNING!

THAT'S CHEATING!

119

CalviN and HobbEs

by WATTERSON

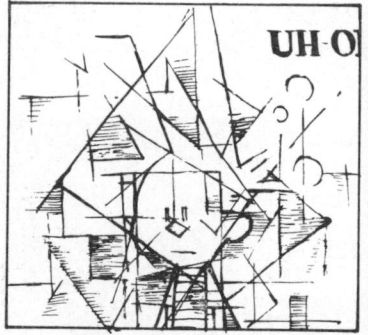

OH NO! EVERYTHING HAS SUDDENLY TURNED NEO-CUBIST!

IT ALL STARTED WHEN CALVIN ENGAGED HIS DAD IN A MINOR DEBATE! SOON CALVIN COULD SEE BOTH SIDES OF THE ISSUE! THEN POOR CALVIN BEGAN TO SEE BOTH SIDES OF *EVERY*THING!

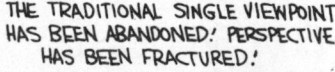

THE TRADITIONAL SINGLE VIEWPOINT HAS BEEN ABANDONED! PERSPECTIVE HAS BEEN FRACTURED!

THE MULTIPLE VIEWS PROVIDE TOO MUCH INFORMATION! IT'S IMPOSSIBLE TO MOVE! CALVIN QUICKLY TRIES TO ELIMINATE ALL BUT ONE PERSPECTIVE!

IT WORKS! THE WORLD FALLS INTO A RECOGNIZABLE ORDER!

YOU'RE STILL WRONG, DAD.

CALVIN and HOBBES

by WATERSON

ANOTHER ONE OF *THESE* DAYS.

UH OH! IN ANOTHER OF LIFE'S MYSTERIOUS QUIRKS, CALVIN FINDS HIMSELF AN INCH TALL ON THE WRITING DESK!

HIS ONLY HOPE IS TO TEAR OFF A SHEET FROM A NEARBY PAD OF PAPER!

AT HIS TINY SIZE, FOLDING THE SHEET IS DIFFICULT, BUT SOON CALVIN'S PATIENCE IS REWARDED!

HE PUSHES OFF AND CATCHES A SMALL THERMAL RISING UP THE FRONT OF THE DESK!

A GUST FROM AN OPEN WINDOW SENDS CALVIN SOARING ACROSS THE HOUSE!

THERE'S DAD! LEAN! LEAN!

YES! CALVIN IS ABLE TO STEER! *THIS* SHOULD GET DAD'S ATTENTION!

I DON'T NEED PARENTS. ALL I NEED IS A RECORDING THAT SAYS, "GO PLAY OUTSIDE!"

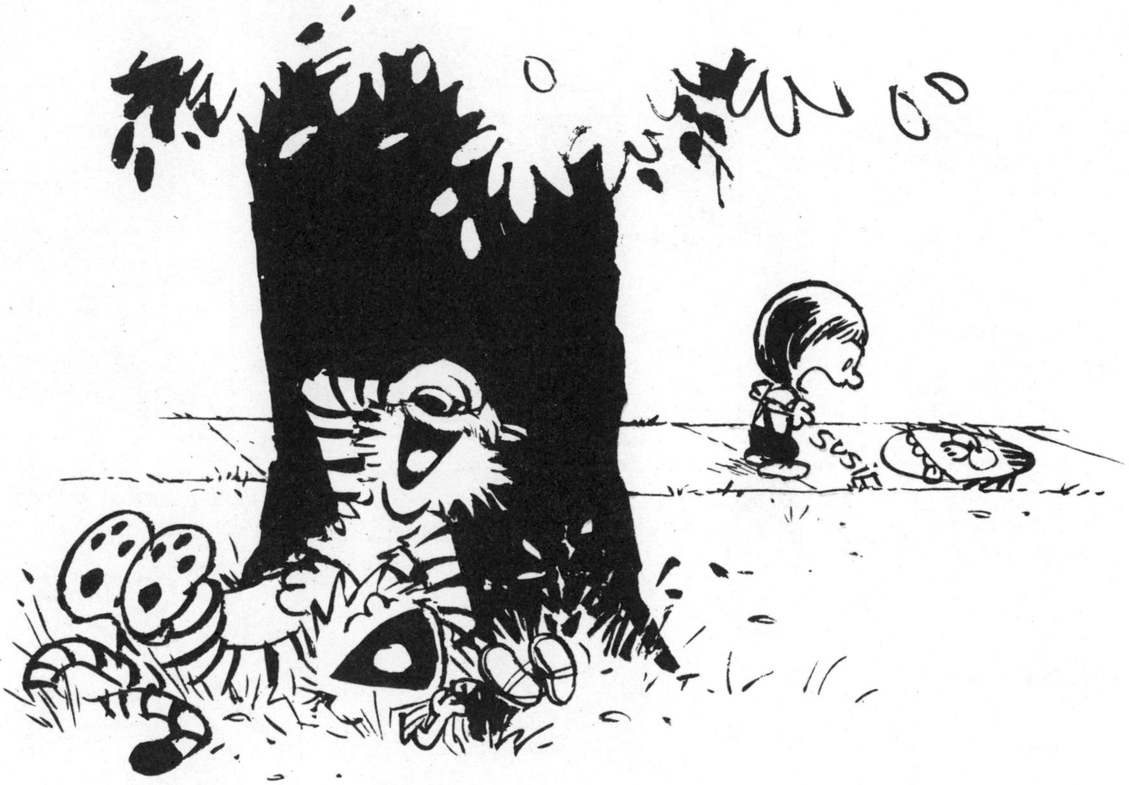
SUSIE

The End